365 DAYS WITH THE PSALMS

365 days with the Psalms

Translation by Joseph Rhymer
Prayers by Alan Robinson

Based on *365 dias com os Salmos,* by Paulo Bazaglia, © Paulus, São Paulo, Brazil

Cover design by Mary Lou Winters. Photo by Tommaso Coscarelli, © Edizioni San Paolo, Cinisello Balsamo, Italy

ST PAULS
Middlegreen, Slough SL3 6BT, United Kingdom
Moyglare Road, Maynooth, Co. Kildare, Ireland

ISBN 085439 514 8

Set by TuKan, High Wycombe

Printed by Redwood Books, Trowbridge

ST PAULS is an activity of the priests and brothers of the Society of St Paul who proclaim the Gospel through the media of social communication

FOREWORD

In his letter to the community in Ephesus (5:19), and again in another to the community in Colossae (3:16), the Apostle Paul tells his readers and listeners to sing hymns, canticles and psalms to God. These people, converts to Christianity, would not have known all the Psalms – there are 150 in the Psalter – but they would have been familiar with those which were recited during the liturgical assembly.

During our Christian worship we also sing certain Psalms, but how familiar are we with them? It is not easy for us in this day and age – even further removed from the world of the Old Testament than those of Paul's time – to pray the Psalms.

Thus we need to enter into the world of the psalmist, placing ourselves before God, just as we are: happy, downcast, angry, moody, full of life, fed-up, unforgiving, dejected, and sometimes, even grateful and thankful.

To pray the Psalms is not simply to recite prayers that were written thousands of years ago. We have to take into account the mentality of the people who wrote the Psalms, the limitations within which they worked, particularly as regards God's plan of salvation.

God did not manifest this plan all at once. As Christians, we believe that the Father revealed himself over thousands of years until, in the fullness of time, he spoke to us definitively through his Son (cf. Heb 1:2).

The psalms therefore are to be read today in the light of the fullness of Christian revelation. Thus, when we read in Psalm 137:8-9: "Blessed he who repays you for what you have done to us, he who seizes your children and dashes them against the rocks", we have to bear in mind the New Testament teaching of Jesus: "Love your enemies, and pray for those who persecute you" (Mt 5:44).

This is where the prayer at the end of each psalm is an aid to our understanding and interpreting it. The prayer will help us to adapt the psalm to our present life-situation and circumstance.

As the reader becomes more familiar with the Psalms, she or he will find them not only to be a mirror of human life but a source of inspiration for one's spiritual life.

1 JANUARY

Yahweh guards the path of the just

PSALM 1

[1] Blessed are those
who reject the advice of the wicked.
They will not walk in the sinner's path
nor take a seat with cynics.
[2] Instead they delight in the law of Yahweh,
and meditate on it day and night.
[3] They are like trees
that grow near a stream,
which bear fruit in season,
whose leaves never wither,
whose plans always prosper.
[4] Not so the wicked,
driven like wind-blown chaff.
[5] The wicked will not stand firm at the judgement,
nor sinners be able to meet with the just.
[6] Yahweh guards the path of the just,
but the path of the wicked is doomed.

O Lord, help me to avoid sin and to love righteousness. Your word and your law are delightful to consider in my heart and mind. I desire to remain constantly beside the stream of your love and to taste the fruit of obedience to your word. May those with evil in their hearts repent and may my sins be blown away like chaff in the wind. No unrighteous thought will stand before the righteousness of your judgement; but I stand before you in hope, because I trust in your word of life. Lead me in your way, O Lord. Amen.

2 JANUARY

Why this rage among the nations?

PSALM 2:1-6

[1] Why this rage among the nations,
futile plotting by the peoples?
[2] Earth's kings take up position,
rulers gather to conspire
against Yahweh and his anointed,
[3] saying, "Let us break their chains
and throw away their fetters!"
[4] The One enthroned in heaven laughs,
Yahweh treats them with derision.
[5] Then he speaks out in his wrath,
terrifies them with his fury.
[6] "I myself enthroned my king
on Zion, my holy mountain."

O Lord, your ways are mysterious to me. Why do you allow nations and peoples to plot evil, and why do you permit the rulers of this world to rebel against you? I know your power is absolute and that your wrathful judgement awaits the wicked. When will you come to curb the powers of this world? You rule as King in the heavenly Zion, O God, and I pray that your kingdom may come upon earth. Amen.

3 JANUARY

You are my son

PSALM 2:7-12

[7] I will proclaim Yahweh's decree.
He said to me, "You are my son,
today I have begotten you.
[8] Ask of me,
I will make the nations your heritage,
the ends of the earth your own.
[9] You will break them with an iron rod,
and shatter them as if they were pots."
[10] Now therefore, you kings, be wise,
be warned, you rulers of the earth.
[11] Serve Yahweh with fear,
pay him homage with trembling,
[12] in case he gets angry,
and destroys you in the way,
for his wrath flares up quickly.
Blessed are all who take refuge in him.

I know, O Lord, that you have a one and only Son, but that you have adopted me also as a son (or daughter). I pray that the kings and rulers of this world may become aware that they also are your sons; and I pray that they will serve you with reverence in the power that you have granted them. May those who turn to you for help be granted the blessing of a safe refuge. Amen.

4 JANUARY

You are the shield

PSALM 3:1-3

[1] My foes are many, O Yahweh;
many there are who rise up against me,
[2] many who say of me,
"God will not save him."
[3] But you are the shield at my side, O Yahweh;
my glory, you hold my head up high.

O God, when the powers of this world seem to be surrounding me and testing me, I pray that you will be with me. Help me to withstand the scorn of unbelievers and to prevail against temptation. Be my shield, and guard me from all harm, by day and by night. Grant me a vision of your glory and hear my prayer, O Lord. Lift my soul heavenwards that I may know that you walk with me. Amen.

5 JANUARY

From Yahweh comes deliverance

PSALM 3:4-8

[4] Whenever I cry to Yahweh
he answers me from his holy hill.
[5] I lie down to sleep,
and I wake up again,
for Yahweh upholds me.
[6] I do not fear forces in thousands and thousands
drawn up against me on every side.
[7] Arise, O Yahweh, save me, my God!

You strike all my foes across the face;
you break the teeth of the wicked ones.
[8] From Yahweh comes deliverance.
May you bless your people.

Sleeping and waking, you strengthen me, O Lord. When I know that you are with me I can face all the difficulties that lie before me. Help me to deal with the problems of each day and to turn the hate of my enemies into love. Arise, O Lord, and save me from all harm. You are my Saviour and in you I find rest. Bless me with your love and hold me in your care, each hour of each day. Amen.

6 JANUARY

You have filled my heart with greater joy

PSALM 4

[1] Answer me when I call to you,
O God, upholder of my right!
You set me free from my distress;
show mercy to me and hear my prayer.
[2] How long will you turn my glory to shame?
How long, you people,
will you love vain words
and seek false gods?
[3] Know that Yahweh takes the faithful to himself;
Yahweh will hear when I call to him.
[4] When you are angry do not sin.
Search your hearts on your beds and be silent.
[5] Make the right offerings
and trust in Yahweh.

[6] There are many who ask,
"Who can give us happiness?"
Let the light of your face
shine upon us, O Yahweh.
[7] You have filled my heart with greater joy
than all their glut of grain and wine.
[8] I shall lie down and sleep in peace, O Yahweh,
for you alone make my life secure.

Give me a portion of your grace, O Lord, and hear my prayer when I cry to you. Help me to leave behind the vanities of this world, that I may turn to you in trustfulness. It is wonderful to know that you are with me as I meditate on your ways. Shine your face upon me each morning as I awake and fill my heart with joy; and each night as I lie down in sleep, grant me safety from harm, and rest in you. Amen.

7 JANUARY

O Yahweh, hear my words

PSALM 5:1-7

[1] O Yahweh, hear my words,
consider my sighing;
[2] listen to my cry for help,
my King and my God.
[3] By morning, O Yahweh, you hear my voice;
by morning, I put my case to you,
and I wait.
[4] You are not a God who takes pleasure in evil;
no wicked can ever be your guest.
[5] The proud will not stand in your eyes;

you hate all those who do wrong.
[6] You destroy the liars;
Yahweh abhors the violent and devious.
[7] But your faithful love is so great
that I may enter your house,
and bow down in awe
at your holy Temple.

Each morning I call to you, O Lord, and I groan at my inadequacy. Prevent me from being self-righteous or boastful in my ways, and guard me in the time of temptation. Rule over my heart and mind, O King of righteousness, and lead me in the paths of truth. May I know your constant love as I enter your house each day. Give me a true spirit of worship and a reverent spirit within me. Amen.

8 JANUARY

Yahweh will bless the righteous

PSALM 5:8-12

[8] In your justice, O Yahweh,
lead me and save me;
because of my enemies make your way plain
for me.
[9] Not a word from their mouth
can anyone trust.
Their hearts plan destruction,
their throats are an open grave,
their tongues speak deceit.
[10] O God, lay their guilt on them;
let their plots be their downfall.

Cast them out for their many sins,
as rebels against you.
[11] But let all who make you their refuge rejoice,
let them sing with joy forever.
Shelter those who love your name;
they rejoice in you.
[12] For you, O Yahweh, will bless the righteous;
your favour surrounds them like a shield.

Go before me, Lord, with your justice and foil the plots of the deceitful. I find faith and hope in you, O God, but the enemies of truth I do not trust. May destructive people who rebel against you find guilt and shame in their hearts; but may those who trust in you find peace and happiness deep within. I love your name, Lord, and I rejoice in the shelter of your righteousness. Bless me and transform me with your love. Amen.

9 JANUARY

Save me because of your faithful love

Psalm 6:1-5

[1] Do not rebuke me, O Yahweh, in your anger,
or punish me in your wrath.
[2] Pity me, O Yahweh, for my strength fails;
O Yahweh, heal me, for my bones are in agony.
[3] My soul is in anguish:
how long, O Yahweh, how long?
[4] Turn, O Yahweh, and save my life,
save me because of your faithful love.
[5] No one remembers you in death;
who could sing your praise in the grave?

Have mercy on me in my weakness, O Lord. Do not judge me according to my deserts, but heal the anguish of my soul as I strive towards you. How long must I be in torment? Have pity on me and save me; replenish me with your constant love. When it seems that death is the end of all things, save my soul and help me to remember that you are the eternal Lord of life. Amen.

10 JANUARY

Yahweh has heard my cry for mercy

PSALM 6:6-10

[6] I am worn out with groaning;
all night my pillow is wet with tears,
my bed is drenched with weeping.
[7] My eyes are weakened by sorrow;
they fail because of all my foes.
[8] Leave me alone, all you who do evil,
for Yahweh has heard the sound of my weeping.
[9] Yahweh has heard my cry for mercy;
Yahweh accepts my prayer.
[10] May all my foes be put to confusion;
may they retreat in sudden disgrace.

Sometimes I am very depressed, Lord. At times, everything and everyone seem to be against me. It is difficult to sleep because my mind is full of problems and in the mornings I am weary and listless. Hear my prayer, O God, and help me in my time of trouble. Fill my heart with the certainty of your presence. Help me to see my problems in the perspective of your eternal love. Abide with me, this day and always. Amen.

11 JANUARY

Judge me, O Yahweh

PSALM 7:1-10

[1] O Yahweh my God, in you I find refuge.
Deliver and save me from all who harass me,
[2] lest they tear at my throat like a lion with prey,
and drag me away with no one to rescue.
[3] O Yahweh my God, if I have done this:
stained my hands with guilt;
[4] repaid friendship with evil;
robbed foe without cause;
[5] let my enemy capture me after pursuing me,
crush my life in the ground
and my honour in dust.
[6] O Yahweh, rise up at my foes in your anger.
Rise up against the rage of my enemies
and let justice be done.
[7] Let all the nations assemble around you,
then sit on your throne
and preside from on high.
[8] Let Yahweh judge the peoples.
Judge me, O Yahweh,
as my innocence merits
and my inner integrity.
[9] O God of all righteousness, searcher of hearts
and minds,
stamp out the wicked;
grant strength to the just.
[10] My shield is God Most High
who saves those who obey him.

Shield me from the powers of evil, Lord. I know that sometimes I am guilty of sin and that I deserve punishment, especially when I have let down my friends. When my honour is at risk, lift me up. May the cause of justice prevail and on the great judgement day may all hearts be searched by your holiness. Yet, O God, to whom can I turn but you? Help me in my weakness and lead me into the ways of goodness and love. Amen.

12 JANUARY

God is a just judge

PSALM 7:11-17

[11] God is a just judge,
whose wrath is consistent.
[12] He will sharpen his sword
if he does not relent;
his drawn bow is strung;
[13] his weapons are deadly,
his arrows are tipped with fire.
[14] All who work evil, pregnant with spite,
whose offspring is mischief,
who give birth to lies:
[15] they dig their own trap and hollow it out,
but they fall in themselves,
[16] caught by their own spite;
their violence recoils on their heads.
[17] I will raise thanks to Yahweh because of his justice,
and sing to the name of Yahweh Most High.

I thank you, Lord, for your constancy in judging wickedness. I know that your will to defeat the forces of evil is implacable and that your power is illimitable. It is certain that mischief makers will receive their just deserts. They will fall into traps of their own making. Their spite will rebound upon themselves. I praise you, O God, for your righteousness and I pray that I may be just in my dealings with others. Amen.

13 JANUARY

How glorious is your name

Psalm 8:1-2

[1] O Yahweh, our Lord,
how glorious is your name
throughout the world!
You have set your glory
above the sky.
[2] You created praise
from the mouths of children
and babes in arms,
to form a fortress against your enemies
and silence the foe and avenger.

I see your glory all around me, Lord, and I praise your name. I praise you with every fibre of my being. I praise you constantly for the love and beauty that you have created for me to enjoy every day. I am like a child before you, O God, but I know that my simple faith is a fortress against evil. No enemy can withstand the strength of your love. Amen.

14 JANUARY

You made him nearly a heavenly being

PSALM 8:3-9

[3] When I look at the sky,
the work of your fingers,
the moon and the stars
which you set in place,
[4] what are people, that you spare a thought for them,
or the child of Adam,
that you care for him?
[5] Yet you made him nearly a heavenly being,
you have crowned him
with glory and beauty.
[6] You have made him lord of the work of your hands
and put all things under his feet:
[7] sheep and cattle, and wild beasts,
[8] the birds in the air, the fish in the sea
and all that moves along oceans' paths.
[9] O Yahweh, our Lord,
how glorious is your name
throughout the earth!

My Lord and my God, how frail I am compared with the works of your creation! I look at the sky and the sun and the moon and the stars and I am amazed that you should care for me. Yet you have given me a beautiful kingdom in which to live. This universe is marvellous to behold and yet, you have created me and given me your work to do. I ask for the wisdom to live my life caringly. I pray for the welfare of the world you have provided. Amen.

15 JANUARY

Yahweh is safety for the oppressed

PSALM 9:1-10

[1] I praise you, O Yahweh, with all my heart,
and tell of all your wonderful deeds;
[2] O Most High, I rejoice and delight in you,
and sing to your name.
[3] My foes turn back;
at your presence they stumble and die,
[4] for you are enthroned as a righteous judge,
and you have upheld my right and my cause.
[5] You rebuked the nations and killed the wicked,
and ruined them for evermore.
[6] The enemy is utterly finished;
you have levelled their cities
and wiped out their memory for evermore.
[7] Yahweh reigns forever,
he has set up his throne for judgement.
[8] He will judge the world in righteousness
and govern the peoples with justice.
[9] Yahweh is safety for the oppressed,
a fortress in troubled times.
[10] Those who know you by name will trust in you;
O Yahweh, you never desert those who
seek you.

Thank you, Lord, for your help in time of trouble. I praise you for all your wonderful deeds. The whole world is in your hands and those nations who are cruel and wicked, I know will receive their just deserts. I pray that I may grow more aware of your majesty and holiness as I try to live my life according to your ways. Hold me in safety, O God, and when my faith falls short, strengthen me. Amen.

16 JANUARY

The hope of the poor never dies

PSALM 9:11-20

[11] Sing praise to Yahweh, enthroned in Zion;
tell the nations what he has done;
[12] the Avenger of Blood does not forget them;
he does not ignore the afflicted's cry.
[13] O Yahweh, see how my foes afflict me;
pull me back from the doors of death
[14] to proclaim your praises and rejoice in your salvation
at the gates of the daughter of Zion.
[15] The nations plunged into the trap they made,
their feet caught in the snare they laid.
[16] Yahweh has made himself known, and has judged,
he has trapped the wicked by the work of their hands.
[17] The wicked go back to the grave,
all nations forgetful of God.
[18] But the needy are not forgotten forever,
the hope of the poor never dies.
[19] Arise, O Yahweh, let not mortals triumph,
let the nations be judged by your face.
[20] O Yahweh, strike them with dread;
let the nations know they are mortal.

I worship you with all my heart, Lord, knowing that you are enthroned in heaven. I know that you care for the afflicted and that you do not forget the poor or the needy. Yet, your power is great enough to crush those nations who forget you. May your judgement fall upon the wicked, and may all oppressed peoples be saved by your love. Show the powers of this world that they are mortal. Hear my prayer, O God. Amen.

17 JANUARY

Do not forget the afflicted

PSALM 10:1-12

[1] Why, O Yahweh, do you keep far off?
Why do you hide in troubled times?
[2] The arrogant wicked hunt down the weak,
and trap them in the schemes they devise.
[3] They boast of the cravings of their hearts;
they bless the greedy and curse Yahweh.
[4] In their pride the wicked ignore him;
God has no place at all in their thoughts.
[5] Their ways are always prosperous;
your judgements are above their heads;
they scoff at all their enemies.
[6] They tell themselves that nothing will shake them,
that happiness lasts without fear of trouble.
[7] Their mouths are all curses, deceit and oppression;
trouble and evil are under their tongues.
[8] They lurk in ambush outside the towns,
watching in secret to murder the innocent.
[9] They lie in wait like a lion in cover;
they lie in wait to catch the helpless,
to catch the helpless enmeshed in their nets.
[10] Their victims are crushed and collapse,

they fall under their power.
[11] They say to themselves that God has forgotten
and covered his face and notices nothing.
[12] Arise, O Yahweh!
Raise your hand, O God,
and do not forget the afflicted.

Sometimes you seem far away, Lord, when the power of evil is rampant. Your ways are ignored by the greedy and deceitful, and they even curse your name. They revel in their prosperity while they oppress the weak. The illusion of false and selfish happiness dominates their minds. I pray, O God, that you will arise and come to the aid of the victims of injustice. May your mighty hand protect them. Amen.

18 JANUARY

Yahweh hears the desires of the poor

PSALM 10:13-18

[13] Why are the wicked allowed to curse God,
and say to themselves he will never take note?
[14] You do notice trouble and grief, O God,
you watch it and take it in hand;
the victims commit themselves to you;
you come to the aid of orphans.
[15] Break the arms of the wicked and evil;
search out evil until there is none.
[16] Yahweh is king for ever and ever;
the heathen will vanish from his land.
[17] You hear, O Yahweh, the desires of the poor;
you give them courage and hear their cry,

[18] you give the verdict for orphan and oppressed,
so that earthborn mortals cause terror no more.

I know, O God, that you take notice of the prayers of those in trouble, especially when they are oppressed by the wicked. I pray that you will remove all evil from this world. May your kingdom come and may it last forever! Give the orphaned and homeless justice, and grant grace and courage to those who falter in their faith. Hear the cry of the afflicted, Lord. Amen.

19 JANUARY

What can the righteous do?

Psalm 11:1-3

[1] In Yahweh I take refuge.
How can you say to me,
"Flee like a bird to the hills!?
[2] See how the wicked bend their bows,
their arrows ready upon the string,
to shoot at the upright from shadows.
[3] When foundations are destroyed,
what can the righteous do?"

What can I do, Lord, when I am surrounded by temptations? I sometimes feel that evil powers are waiting to capture me and I cannot escape. If the moral foundations of society are collapsing, where can I come for help? I turn to you now, O God, and seek refuge with you. Guard me from the darts of Satan and keep me safe, this day and always. Amen.

20 JANUARY

Yahweh is righteous

Psalm 11:4-7

[4] Yahweh is in his holy Temple;
Yahweh has set firm his heavenly throne.
His eye is on the human race;
he takes its measure at a glance.
[5] Yahweh tests both just and wicked;
he hates all those devoted to violence.
[6] He showers the wicked with fire and sulphur;
their reward will be a scorching wind.
[7] Yahweh is righteous, devoted to justice,
his face looks with favour on the just.

Only your foundations are sure, O God. Only in you lie the certainties of justice and righteousness. I feel you are searching me to my depths and I pray that you will strengthen me in the time of testing. Your presence is like a purifying fire within me, O God, and I stand in fear before the scorching wind of your holiness. I pray that you will abide within me to change me, according to your will. Amen.

21 JANUARY

For the faithful are no more

Psalm 12

[1] Help, O Yahweh, for the faithful are no more;
the faithful have vanished from among the
people.

[2] Neighbour tells lies to neighbour,
and speaks smooth words from a devious heart.

[3] May Yahweh cut off each flattering lip
and every boastful tongue,

[4] from those who say,
"Our tongues are our strength
and our lips are our allies,
so who is our master?"

[5] Yahweh says,
"The weak are oppressed,
the needy are groaning,
so I will arise!
I will grant them the safety
for which they long."

[6] The words of Yahweh are unalloyed,
like silver refined in a crucible,
like silver purified seven times over.

[7] O Yahweh, you will always watch over us,
you will guard us from people like that.

[8] The wicked prowl on every side
when people honour what is vile.

Where are your faithful followers, O Lord? Where are those who seek truth and justice? Neighbours tell deceitful lies to each other and the arrogant boast of their own power. But your word is truth and your promises are sure. Help the needy and weak and grant them a safe haven. Watch over them and watch over me in my weakness, O God. Be my shield in this wicked world. Amen.

22 JANUARY

How long, O Yahweh?

PSALM 13

[1] How long, O Yahweh, will you forget me?
    Forever?
How long will you turn your face from me?
[2] How long must I nurse rebellious thoughts,
    and sorrow of heart throughout the day?
How long is the foe to dominate me?
[3] O Yahweh my God, look down and answer me,
give light to my eyes,
    or death is my sleep.
[4] My foe will say, "I have overthrown him,"
    and my enemies rejoice at my fall.
[5] But I put trust in your faithful love,
    my heart will rejoice in your saving help.
[6] I will sing to Yahweh
    for he has granted all I desire.

Why is it, O Lord, that you seem to turn away from me? How long must I wait before you answer my prayer? I am constantly sorrowful and my unhappiness is taking control of me. Evil powers are waiting to overcome my spirit. Yet I know that you are the light of my life, so I wait patiently for your saving help. I trust in your never-failing love, O God, and I long to sing your praise. Amen.

23 JANUARY

Yahweh looks down from heaven

Psalm 14:1-3

[1] The fool has said in his heart,
"There is no God!"
They are depraved and their deeds are vile;
not one of them does any good.
[2] Yahweh looks down from heaven
on all the human race
to see if any are wise,
if any seek after God.
[3] All have turned away,
they have all become corrupt,
not one of them does right,
not even one.

When doubts assail me, O God, give me your grace. I look around and it seems that many do not know you. People do terrible things to each other. Good deeds are rare and wickedness seems to prevail. Yet you know every heart, Lord, and you know that some people do seek you. I pray that you will reveal yourself to the faithful, that my faith may be renewed. Amen.

24 JANUARY

God is with the just

Psalm 14:4-7

[4] Will the wicked never learn?
They devour my people like bread,

and never call to Yahweh.
[5] They will be gripped in terror,
for God is with the just.
[6] You may mock the plans of the poor
but Yahweh is their refuge.
[7] O that Israel's salvation
would come from Zion!
When Yahweh restores his people's fortunes,
let Jacob rejoice
and Israel be glad.

The people of God are persecuted by the wicked. The poor are mocked by the godless. I pray, Lord, that you will come from heaven to restore your people. You are my refuge and strength and I will rejoice in your salvation. Show the faithful your love, O God, and give justice to the persecuted. May your people be joyful always. You are my fortress and I will praise you forever. Amen.

25 JANUARY

O Yahweh, who may stay in your tent?

PSALM 15

[1] O Yahweh, who may stay in your tent?
Who may live on your holy hill?
[2] Whoever lives blamelessly,
whoever acts honestly,
whoever speaks truth from the heart,
[3] who keeps guard on his tongue,
does his neighbour no wrong,
casts no slurs on his fellows,

[4] who despises the vile,
honours those who fear Yahweh,
stands by oaths to his cost;
[5] who lends without usury,
takes no bribes against the innocent.
Whoever does these things
will never be shaken.

O Lord, thank you for the guidance you have given me through your holy word. I would like to live in your kingdom from day to day and, when I leave this life, I would like to dwell with you forever. Give me the strength to behave uprightly and to keep my word, even if it is to my disadvantage. If you walk with me I know that I will stand firm and nothing will shake my faith. Amen.

26 JANUARY

My inheritance is lovely

PSALM 16:1-6

[1] Protect me, O God, for in you I take refuge.
[2] I said to Yahweh, "You are my Lord;
from you alone comes all I hold good."
[3] I am filled with delight by the noble ones,
the godly ones of the earth.
[4] Those who follow other gods
will find that their sorrows increase.
I will not pour their libations of blood,
nor take their names on my lips.
[5] O Yahweh, my birthright, my cup;
you have made my portion secure.

[6] The division of land gave me pleasant places,
my inheritance is lovely indeed.

Those who live good lives in the light of your goodness, O God, are a beacon to me as I endeavour to live my own life. I know that those who follow false pathways will come to no good and I pray that I may not be led by them into wrongdoing. You are my refuge and my life. In you alone will I find my true inheritance. To know your love and goodness is wonderful indeed! Amen.

27 JANUARY

You will teach me the path of life

PSALM 16:7-11

[7] I bless Yahweh, who counsels me,
even at night my heart instructs me.
[8] I keep Yahweh always before me;
with him at my right hand
nothing can shake me.
[9] So my heart is glad, and my spirit rejoices;
my body also will rest secure;
[10] you will not abandon me to the grave,
nor let your faithful one see decay.
[11] You will teach me the path of life;
your presence brings unending joy,
your right hand grants delight forever.

Guide me in all things, O Lord, and teach me the path of eternal life. If you are with me, who can make me tremble? I rejoice in your love and I feel safe with you by my side. I know that the faithful will meet you in heaven and I pray that I may reach your safe refuge. Fill my heart with gladness and show me the way I ought to go. Amen.

28 JANUARY

Prove to me your faithful love

PSALM 17:1-7

[1] O Yahweh, hear my righteous plea;
pay attention to my cry;
hear my prayer
– it is not from lying lips.
[2] May my vindication come from you;
may your eyes see what is right.
[3] You probed and watched me all night long;
your tests have proved me innocent.
[4] As for human deeds,
guided by your spoken word,
I avoided the path the violent tread.
[5] My steps stay firmly on your way;
my feet secure, I never slip.
[6] O God, I call; you answer me.
Listen to me; hear my words.
[7] Prove to me your faithful love,
you who save by your right hand
all who seek you when attacked.

I thank you for listening to my prayers, O Lord. I know that so often you have steered me away from danger or from unwise actions. You know me through and through and all my life is open to you. Though the path may be steep and stony, I pray that you will guide my every footstep. Show me your constant love, O God, and I shall be saved from all harm. Amen.

29 JANUARY

Hide me in the shadow of your wings

PSALM 17:8-15

[8] Guard me as the apple of your eye;
hide me in the shadow of your wings,
[9] from the wicked who attack me,
as deadly foes close in on me.
[10] With hardened hearts and arrogant cries,
[11] they press me hard, they hem me in,
watching close to bring me down,
[12] like a lion marking prey,
a young lion crouched in cover.
[13] Confront them, O Yahweh; bring them down.
Save me from the wicked by your sword,
[14] from them, by your hand, O Yahweh;
from people of the world,
whose reward is in their lives.
You fill the stomach of those you cherish;
their offspring will have plenty
to store up wealth for their children.
[15] But my plea is just; I shall see your face;
my blessing will be seeing you when I awake.

Under your wing I pray, and under your eye I hope to live each day of my life. Keep me from all harm, Lord, especially when it seems that evil powers are all around me. Confront the enemies of righteousness with your mighty power, and grant the faithful wealth of spirit.

May those who pursue wickedness find their own reward, but give justice to your people. Above all, O God, when life is done and all conflict is over, I pray for the wonderful blessing of seeing you face to face. Amen.

30 JANUARY

God is my shield, my power of salvation

PSALM 18:1-5

[1] I love you, O Yahweh, my strength.
[2] My rock is Yahweh, my fortress, my saviour,
my God, the rock where I find safety.
He is my shield, my power of salvation,
my stronghold.
[3] When I call upon Yahweh, who merits all praise,
I am saved from my foes.
[4] The bonds of death entangled me,
destruction swallowed me,
[5] the ropes of the grave surrounded me,
the snares of death lay in my path.

You are my rock and my salvation, O Lord, and I love you with my whole heart. Be my shield in the face of danger and temptation: be my stronghold when I am afraid. I know that you hear my prayer and I ask you for your help whenever I am faced by the powers of evil. Although death lies ahead, I trust in your word of life. O God, you are above all praise, but in my own quiet way I praise you. Amen.

31 JANUARY

The Most High uttered his voice

Psalm 18:6-15

[6] In my anguish I called on Yahweh,
I cried to my God for help.
From his Temple he heard my voice,
and my cry reached his ears.
[7] The earth quaked and trembled,
the roots of the mountains shook,
they quaked because he was angry.
[8] Smoke went up from his nostrils,
devouring fire came from his mouth
and blazing coals poured out.
[9] He split the heavens and came down
with dark clouds beneath his feet.
[10] He flew on mounted cherubim,
and soared on the wings of the wind.
[11] He made darkness into a covering
and storm clouds into a canopy.
[12] His radiance broke through the clouds
with hailstones and bolts of fire.
[13] Yahweh thundered in heaven;
the Most High uttered his voice:
hailstones and bolts of fire.
[14] He fired his arrows and scattered them;
lightning flashes routed them.
[15] The valleys of the sea were revealed.
The foundations of the world were laid bare
by your rebuke, O Yahweh,
by the blast of the breath of your nostrils.

Your glory is revealed in the powers of nature, Lord. The mountains shake at your command. Thunder and lightning show your majesty upon the clouds of the storm. You raise up the oceans in tumult and the foundations of the world are bared to your view. Yet, powerless as I am, I cry to you for help, O God. May my prayer be heard and may your infinite power save me from all harm. Amen.

1 FEBRUARY

He reached from the heights to grasp me

PSALM 18:16-23

[16] He reached from the heights to grasp me,
    and drew me out of deep waters.
[17] He saved me from foes, strong foes,
from my foes
    when they grew too strong for me.
[18] My day of disaster came when they attacked,
    but Yahweh came to my aid.
[19] He brought me into an open place,
    he rescued me because he loves me.
[20] Yahweh gave me my just recognition,
    he rewarded me for my innocent hands;
[21] for I have kept the ways of Yahweh,
    and have not wickedly left my God.
[22] All his judgements are there before me,
    I have not turned from his decrees,
[23] I came into his presence blameless
    and kept myself from sin.

Often you have saved me from my own folly, or from my enemies, O Lord, and I thank you for your wondrous grace. Your love for me is above all human loves, and I pray that your watchfulness will keep me from straying from the path of innocence. I have promised to hold to your laws and to keep myself free from sin. I am aware of my weakness and pray for the strength of your Spirit within me. Amen.

2 FEBRUARY

You save the humble

Psalm 18:24-29

[24] Therefore Yahweh rewarded me
according to my righteousness,
for the cleanness of my hands.
[25] With the faithful you show you are faithful,
with the blameless you are blameless,
[26] with the pure you show you are pure,
but with the crafty you show you are shrewd.
[27] You save the humble,
but bring down proud eyes.
[28] You light my lamp;
Yahweh my God
brings light to my darkness.
[29] Indeed, by you I can crush an army,
and by my God I leap over a wall.

I know, O Lord, that you reward everyone according to his (her) actions. The faithful and righteous will know your faithfulness and righteousness: the crafty and the proud will know your wisdom in judgement. You are the lamp by which I walk and your presence illuminates my darkness. When you are with me I am empowered to do more than I had ever imagined. Shine your lamp before my feet, O God. Amen.

3 FEBRUARY

The way of God is without blame

PSALM 18:30-42

[30] The way of God is without blame,
the word of Yahweh is without flaw.
He alone is the shield
of all who take refuge in him.
[31] For who is God, but Yahweh?
And who is a rock, but our God?
[32] It is God who girds me with strength
and makes my way secure.
[33] He makes my feet like the feet of a deer,
so that I stand secure on the heights.
[34] He trains my hands for the battle,
my arms to bend a bow of bronze.
[35] You give me your victory shield;
your right hand holds me up;
you stoop to make me great.
[36] You widen the path beneath me,
so that my feet do not slip.
[37] I chased my foes and caught them,
and did not turn back until they were dead.
[38] I crushed them never to rise again;
they fell beneath my feet.
[39] You armed me with strength for the fight,
you made my attackers bend beneath me;
[40] you made my enemies run from me,
and I destroyed my foes.
[41] They cried for help, but none could save them;
they cried to Yahweh but he did not answer.
[42] I beat them as fine as dust in the wind;
I threw them out like mud in the streets.

Your word is perfect, O Lord. You alone are my shield and defender. I pray that you will strengthen my arm and that you will guide my feet. May the path before me be broad and well marked so that I do not fall. With you by my side, I will fight the powers of evil and defeat the enemies of truth and goodness. Be my rock and my refuge, O God, through all the chances and changes of my life. Amen.

4 FEBRUARY

I will praise you among the nations

PSALM 18:43-50

[43] You have set me free from attacks by the people,
you have placed me at the head of nations;
[44] as soon as they hear of me they obey,
and foreigners come before me cringing.
[45] Foreigners all grow faint of heart,
and come with trembling from their
strongholds.
[46] Yahweh lives! Blessed be my Rock!
May God my Saviour be exalted!
[47] He is the God who gives me vengeance,
and makes the nations subject to me.
[48] He delivers me from all my foes.
You raised me high above my enemies,
you delivered me from violent people.
[49] For this, O Yahweh,
I will praise you among the nations;
I will sing praises to your name.
[50] He grants his king great victories,
shows faithful love to his anointed,
David and his heirs forever.

I pray, O Lord, that the rulers of this world may learn the wisdom of heaven. May they rule in equity and peace under your guidance. All nations will praise your name and will eventually subscribe to your love, for your will cannot be opposed. When that day comes, O God, your anointed King will reign throughout the whole of creation. I praise you mightily for the wonder and the mystery of your ways. Amen.

5 FEBRUARY

The glory of God is no speech nor words

PSALM 19:1-6

[1] The heavens declare the glory of God;
the skies proclaim his handiwork;
[2] one day tells the next day;
night passes on the knowledge to night.
[3] There is no speech nor words,
and not a sound is heard,
[4] but their voice goes out to all the earth,
and their words to the end of the world.
He has pitched a tent for the sun in the heavens,
[5] which comes like a bridegroom from his chamber,
like a champion running the course with joy.
[6] It rises at one end of the heavens
and runs its circuit to the other;
nothing is hidden from its heat.

My heart lifts with joy, O Lord, when I look upon your creation and all its beauty. Time and space are your handiwork and your glory fills the universe. Your light encompasses the earth and the heavens, and nothing is hidden from your eyes. I thank you for the gift of this marvellous being, for the senses which speak to me of your presence in all that I experience. My God, I give thanks to you for all your good gifts. Amen.

6 FEBRUARY

Yahweh's precepts are right

PSALM 19:7-14

[7] Yahweh's law is perfect, reviving the soul;
Yahweh's statutes are sure,
making the simple wise.
[8] Yahweh's precepts are right,
giving joy to the heart.
Yahweh's commands are right,
giving light to the eyes.
[9] The fear of Yahweh is pure,
and lasts forever.
Yahweh's judgements are true,
and every one is just.
[10] They are more desirable than gold,
even than much fine gold;
they are sweeter also than honey,
than honey from the comb.
[11] Through them your servant is warned;
keeping them brings great reward.
[12] Who can detect his own failings?
Clear me from hidden faults.
[13] Preserve your servant from pride;
do not let it gain hold of me.
Then I shall be guiltless,
and free from any great sin.

[14] Let the words of my mouth
and the thoughts of my heart
be pleasing to you, O Yahweh,
my rock and redeemer.

The laws of your love are growing within me, O Lord, and your word is my inward light. To follow your ways in peace and reverence is my deepest desire. Yet, I am aware of my many faults and I pray that you will help me to grow closer to you each day. May everything I think, or speak or do, be acceptable to you, my Rock and my Redeemer. Amen.

7 FEBRUARY

May Yahweh grant the desire of your heart

PSALM 20:1-5

[1] May Yahweh hear you in time of trouble,
may the God of Jacob's name protect you!
[2] May he send you help from the sanctuary,
and support you from Zion.
[3] May he remember all your offerings,
and delight in your sacrifices!
[4] May he grant the desire of your heart
and make all your plans succeed!
[5] Then we shall hail your victory,
and lift up our flags in the name of God.
May Yahweh grant all that you ask!

In this temple of my body, O Lord, I pray to you for help and guidance. Hear my cry in times of trouble and be with me in all my endeavours. My wish is to live in accord with your love, but I pray also for victory over my selfishness. I praise your name, O God, and I am joyful in your presence. May my worship be acceptable before you and may my requests conform with your will. Amen.

8 FEBRUARY

We trust in the name of Yahweh our God

PSALM 20:6-9

[6] Now I know that Yahweh saves his anointed,
and answers him from his holy heaven
with the saving might of his right hand.
[7] Some trust in chariots, and some in horses,
but we trust in the name of Yahweh our God.
[8] They all crumple and fall,
while we rise up and stand firm.
[9] O Yahweh, save the king,
and answer us when we call.

I trust in you, O Lord, and not in the powers of this world. Empires may pass away, but your word stands eternally. I know that you listen to all who pray to you and that you are ready to help those who turn to you in despair. When I am despondent, I pray that you will give me courage. When I am full of pride, I pray that you will give me humility. I praise you with my whole heart, O God of all power and might. Amen.

9 FEBRUARY

The king rejoices in the triumphs you give

PSALM 21:1-7

[1] O Yahweh, the king rejoices in your power;
how great is his joy in the triumphs you give!
[2] You have given him his heart's desire,
and have not denied the request of his lips.
[3] You came to meet him with blessings of wealth,
and placed a crown of pure gold on his head.
[4] He asked for life, and you gave it to him,
length of days forever and ever.
[5] His glory is great through the help you give;
you invest him with splendour and majesty.
[6] You give him blessings which last forever,
you make him glad with the joy of your presence.
[7] For the king trusts in Yahweh;
the Most High's faithful love
will save him from falling.

I thank you, O Lord, for giving me as my birthright a kingdom of body, mind and spirit. I thank you also for the wealth of this kingdom in all its wonder and miraculous beauty. You crowned me with life and you gave me countless blessings. I trust in you, O God, and I praise you for the constant love which surrounds me. Guard me on my path to your city, night and day, until I leave this kingdom behind, to enter your even more wonderful kingdom of heaven. Amen.

10 FEBRUARY

Rise in your power, O Yahweh!

PSALM 21:8-13

[8] Your hand will reach all your foes;
your right hand will seize your enemies.
[9] You will make them like a blazing furnace
in the day when you appear.
Yahweh will swallow them up in his anger,
and fire will consume them.
[10] You will rid the earth of their offspring,
and root out their children
from all the nations.
[11] If they plot evil against you,
and plan many wicked schemes,
they will not succeed.
[12] For you will put them to flight
when you aim at them with your bow.
[13] Rise in your power, O Yahweh!
We will sing in praise of your might.

I know, O Lord, that you have the power to defeat all the enemies of your glorious kingdom. I pray that all the evil schemes of the wicked will be consumed in the fire of your judgement. I await the day of your coming when your kingdom will be revealed upon earth as it is in heaven. Arise, O God, and defeat the powers of Satan! I praise you for your eternal power and glory. Amen.

11 FEBRUARY

Why have you forsaken me?

PSALM 22:1-11

[1] My God, O my God,
why have you forsaken me?
Why are you far from saving me,
so far from hearing my groans?
[2] O my God,
by day I call but you do not answer;
and by night, but I get no respite.
[3] Yet you are the Holy One,
enthroned in Israel's praises.
[4] Our fathers put their trust in you,
they trusted, and you made them free.
[5] They cried to you and were saved;
they trusted you and were not put to shame.
[6] But I am a worm, not a human;
the scorn of mankind and contempt of
the people.
[7] All who see me jeer at me,
they sneer at me and wag their heads:
[8] "He trusts in Yahweh; let Yahweh save him!
Let him deliver him,
because he loves him!"
[9] Yet you were the one
who brought me from the womb;
you kept me safe on my mother's breast.
[10] At my birth I was put in your care;
from my mother's womb you have been
my God.
[11] Do not stay far from me;
trouble is near to me;
there is no help.

Sometimes, O Lord, I feel that you have forsaken me and left me to my own devices. Yet, even then, deep in my heart, I know that you are eternally the Holy God who is never far away. I place my trust in you and I pray that you will set me free from the bonds of despair. I know that you have cared for me from the time of my birth and that you have watched over every step of my way. Stay close to me, O God, and be my help in time of trouble. Amen.

12 FEBRUARY

Come quickly to my aid!

PSALM 22:12-21

[12] Many bulls are surrounding me,
strong bulls of Bashan
are circling around me.
[13] Roaring and ravening lions
open their jaws at me.
[14] My strength drains like water,
all my bones are disjointed.
My heart is like wax:
it has melted within me.
[15] My strength is dry as earthenware,
my tongue sticks to my mouth
and I am lying in the dust of death.
[16] Dogs have surrounded me;
an evil group has encircled me;
they have pierced my hands and my feet.
[17] I can count all my bones
while they look on and gloat.
[18] They share out my garments

and toss for my clothes.

[19] But you, O Yahweh, do not stay aloof;
come quickly, my Strength, to my aid!

[20] Save my soul from the sword,
my only life from the grip of the dogs.

[21] Deliver me from the lions' mouths,
save me from wild oxen's horns.

The wild beasts of temptation surround me, O Lord, and the dogs of Satan pursue me. I feel drained of strength and my heart melts with fear. Evil powers gloat over me as if they are gambling for my very spirit. But you, O God, are my protector. Come speedily to my help! Save my soul from the jaws of hell. Abide with me, O God, in my time of trial, my Redeemer and my Saviour. Amen.

13 FEBRUARY

He has not spurned the poverty of the poor

PSALM 22:22-31

[22] I will speak of your fame to my brothers;
I will praise you in the great assembly.

[23] Praise him, all you who fear Yahweh!
Honour him, you offspring of Jacob!
Revere him, you children of Israel!

[24] For he has not spurned or ignored
the poverty of the poor.
He has not turned his face from him
but has heard his cry for help.

[25] You inspire me with praise in the crowded
assembly;

I fulfil my vows before all who fear you.
[26] The poor will eat to the full;
they who seek Yahweh will praise him.
May your hearts live forever!
[27] May the whole world remember
and turn to Yahweh.
May all families of nations
do homage before him,
[28] for royal power belongs to Yahweh
and he it is who rules the nations.
[29] All who prosper on earth will feast and worship;
all who are mortal will kneel before him,
all who cannot give themselves life.
[30] Their children will serve him;
the child of the future
will hear about Yahweh;
[31] his salvation will be proclaimed
to a nation not yet born,
that he has fulfilled it.

I praise you, O Lord, with my brothers and sisters of the faith. Honour and reverence are due to your holiness and all embracing love. I pray for your help in keeping my vow to serve you all the days of my life. I long for the day when the whole world will acknowledge your name and everyone will taste the bread of life. Into your hands, O God, I commend our children's children, that they may know your love. Amen.

14 FEBRUARY

My shepherd is Yahweh

Psalm 23

[1] My shepherd is Yahweh,
I want for nothing.
[2] He lets me lie in fields of grass;
he leads me by quiet streams
[3] to revive my spirit.
He guides me in paths of righteousness
as befits his name.
[4] If I walked in the dark vale of death,
I would fear no danger
with you at my side;
your staff and crook both comfort me.
[5] You set a table for me
in the presence of my foes;
you have poured fine oils on my head
and my cup brims over.
[6] Goodness and faithful love
will follow me all my life.
I make my home in Yahweh's house forever.

When you are watching me, Lord, you lead me through meadows beside quiet streams and you uplift my spirit. I know I am on the right path if you are beside me and even if the valley of death lies ahead, I am not afraid, because you are my constant support. My cup of happiness is filled to the brim, O God, because you have invited me to your feast. Your love is so wonderful that I wish to make my home with you forever. Amen.

15 FEBRUARY

Who may go up the mountain of Yahweh?

PSALM 24:1-6

[1] The earth is Yahweh's and all it contains,
the world and all who live there;
[2] he laid its foundations on the seas
and fixed it firm on the waters beneath.
[3] Who may go up the mountain of Yahweh?
Who may stand in his holy place?
[4] The clean handed and pure hearted,
who does not set his heart on falsehood
or swear an oath deceitfully.
[5] Such will receive a blessing from Yahweh,
and justice from the Saviour God.
[6] Such is the fortune of those who seek,
who seek your face, O God of Jacob.

O Lord, Creator of the universe and all it contains, how may I dwell with you in heaven? With your help, I will try to be pure and guiltless, and I shall endeavour to walk in the ways of truth. I seek you daily, O God, and I long to learn your love. I pray for your blessing on all I think or speak or do; and though I do not deserve your love, I hope for your salvation. Amen.

16 FEBRUARY

He is the King of Glory

PSALM 24:7-10

[7] Lift up your heads, you gates,
and open up, eternal doors,

that the King of Glory may enter!
[8] Who is he, this king of glory?
Yahweh, strong and mighty!
Yahweh, mighty in battle!
[9] Lift up your heads, you gates,
and open up, eternal doors,
that the King of Glory may enter!
[10] Who is he, this king of glory?
Yahweh of Hosts!
He is the King of Glory.

Your presence is wonderful to me, O Lord. I pray that a reflection of your glory may shine upon my worship, that I may know more clearly your majesty and power. Grant that I may perceive even a hint of your holiness through my devotions. You are my King for ever, O God, and I open my life to you in the hope that you may open the gates of heaven for me. Amen.

17 FEBRUARY

Yahweh is good and righteous

PSALM 25:1-15

[1] To you, O Yahweh,
I lift up my soul.
[2] I put my trust in you, my God;
do not let me be put to shame,
nor let my foes exult over me.
[3] None who hope in you
will ever be put to shame;
let them be shamed
who break faith without cause.

[4] Make your ways known to me, O Yahweh,
and teach me your paths.
[5] Lead me in your truth and teach me,
for you are God my saviour,
and I wait for you all the day long.
[6] O Yahweh, remember your faithful love and mercy,
for they have been yours forever.
[7] Do not remember the sins of my youth
and my transgressions;
but remember me in your faithful love,
and your goodness, O Yahweh.
[8] Yahweh is good and righteous;
he teaches sinners to go his way.
[9] He leads the humble in what is right,
and teaches them his way.
[10] Unfailing in love and constancy
are the ways of Yahweh
for those who observe
the demands of his covenant.
[11] For the sake of your name, O Yahweh,
forgive my sin, however great.
[12] Who is the person who fears Yahweh?
He will teach such the chosen path.
[13] It will lead to days spent prosperously,
and the children will inherit the land.
[14] Yahweh makes friends with those who fear him,
and makes his covenant known to them.
[15] My eyes are always fixed on Yahweh,
for he will free my feet from the snare.

I lift up my heart in trust to you, O Lord. I search the mystery of your ways and pray that you will teach me the right path. I repent of my sins and I long for your mercy and faithful love to touch me. Your love never fails and you are a friend to those who seek you in sincerity and truth. I look for you, O God, and I pray that you will keep me from falling into Satan's snare. Amen.

18 FEBRUARY

Be kind to me

PSALM 25:16-22

16 Turn to me and be kind to me,
  for I am alone and distressed.
17 Relieve the troubles of my heart,
  save me from my anguish.
18 Look at my anguish and pain,
  and forgive me all my sins.
19 See how my foes have increased,
  and how violently they hate me.
20 Guard my life and rescue me;
  let me not be put to shame,
  for you are where I find refuge.
21 Let virtue and justice protect me;
  in you I put my trust.
22 Deliver Israel, O God,
  from all their troubles.

When I am alone and greatly troubled, O Lord, turn to me in your loving kindness and save me from my distress. Guard my footsteps in case I should be tempted to take the wrong path. My refuge is with you alone and in you I put my trust. I reach to you in faith, O God, and I pray for your deliverance from my difficulties. May your light shine before me each day. Amen.

19 FEBRUARY

Prove me, O Yahweh

PSALM 26:1-5

[1] O Yahweh, be my judge,
for I have led a blameless life;
I have trusted in Yahweh
without wavering.
[2] Prove me, O Yahweh, and try me;
test my heart and my mind.
[3] For your faithful love is before my eyes,
and I live my life by your truth.
[4] I have not sat with devious people;
I will not mix with hypocrites.
[5] I hate the company of sinners;
I will not sit with evil people.

If my trust in you should waver, O Lord, or if my faith should grow dim, I pray that you will come to me to renew my being. I long to abide in your constant love and to live according to the truths you have revealed in your holy word. When I am tested, prove me strong in your grace, O God. Help me to avoid temptation and sin and to pursue purity and holiness of life, this day and always. Amen.

20 FEBRUARY

Redeem me, Lord

PSALM 26:6-12

[6] I wash my hands with innocence,
to go about your altar, O Yahweh,

[7] telling all your mighty acts,
    proclaiming them with thankful voice.
[8] O Yahweh, I love your dwelling place,
    the place in which your glory lives.
[9] Do not cast me out with sinners,
    my life with them who thirst for blood,
[10] whose hands are stained with guilt,
    their right hands filled with bribes.
[11] But I will lead a blameless life;
    redeem me; show me graciousness.
[12] I take my stand on solid ground,
    to bless the Lord in great assemblies.

I love to worship you, O Lord, and I praise you for all your wonderful deeds. I glorify your name as it echoes throughout the universe, for the whole of creation is your temple. I pray for grace to lead a blameless life. Forgive my past sins and help me to mend my ways. When you are with me, O God, I know that my feet are on a sure pathway. I thank you for the revelation of your love. Amen.

21 FEBRUARY

Whom should I fear?

PSALM 27:1-6

[1] Yahweh is my light and salvation,
    whom should I fear?
Yahweh is the fortress of my life,
    whom should I dread?
[2] When the wicked advance against me
    to eat up my flesh;

my enemies, my foes will be the ones who fall.

[3] If I am trapped by an army,
my heart will not fear;
if war breaks out against me,
I will still not be worried.

[4] I only ask one thing of Yahweh,
this is what I seek:
to dwell in Yahweh's house
all my life long,
to gaze on Yahweh's beauty
and to seek him in his temple.

[5] For in the evil day
he will keep me safe in his house,
he will hide me in his tent
and set me high on a rock.

[6] Then I will hold my head high
above the foes who surround me;
I shall fill his tent with shouts of joy
as I sacrifice to him;
I will sing and play music to Yahweh.

While you are my light, O Lord, I shall fear nothing. While you are my fortress, I shall not falter. When evil powers surround me my spirit will be strong, for I know that you are with me. I wish only to be with you, to praise your beauty and your holiness. To dwell in your house is to live in safety: to enter your tent is the joy of all joys. O God, I praise you with all my heart and soul. Amen.

22 FEBRUARY

I shall see Yahweh's goodness

Psalm 27:7-14

[7] O Yahweh, listen when I call,
pity me and answer me.
[8] My heart tells me to seek his face;
your face, O Yahweh, will I seek.
[9] Do not turn away from me,
nor in your anger dismiss your servant;
you have always been my help.
Never leave me, never desert me,
O God, my Saviour.
[10] Though my father and mother forsake me,
Yahweh will receive me.
[11] O Yahweh, teach me your way;
lead me by a level path
because of my enemies.
[12] Do not leave me to the will of my foes,
for lying witnesses rise against me,
breathing out malice.
[13] I still believe firmly
that I shall see Yahweh's goodness
in the land of the living.
[14] Wait for Yahweh;
be strong and take heart
and wait for Yahweh.

Hear me, O Lord, when I call, and do not turn your face away from me. Your love is greater than the love parents have for their children, so I know you will never desert me when troubles come. Do not leave me in the hands of evil forces, but lead me by your eternal light onto a straight path. I wait for you, O God, for my strength is in you. Amen.

23 FEBRUARY

Do not take me away with the wicked

PSALM 28:1-5

[1] O Yahweh, my rock, I call to you,
do not refuse to listen to me,
for if you do not reply to me,
I will be like those who go down to the grave.
[2] Hear the sound of my prayer
as I call to you for help,
as I raise up my hands
towards your Most Holy Place.
[3] Do not take me away with the wicked,
with those who do evil,
who speak peace to their neighbours
with malice in their hearts.
[4] Repay them for what they have done
and for their evil work;
repay them for their handiwork
and give them what they deserve.
[5] They show no respect for Yahweh's works
or what his hands have done;
so he will tear them down
and never rebuild them.

You are my rock, O Lord, and I build my life upon you. I praise you in the deep heart of my prayerfulness, and I await your word. I pray that I may have the power to avoid wicked ways and that my mind may be filled with sincerity and truth. Tear down any sins or hypocrisies which lodge themselves in me, O God, and mould me according to your will. Amen.

24 FEBRUARY

Yahweh is my strength

PSALM 28:6-9

[6] Praise be to Yahweh,
for he has heard the sound of my prayer.
[7] Yahweh is my strength and shield;
my heart trusts him and I find help.
With joyful heart
I sing thanks to him.
[8] Yahweh is his people's strength,
a saving fortress for his anointed.
[9] Save your people and bless your inheritance,
be their shepherd and bear them forever.

I praise you with heart and soul, O Lord, for listening to my prayer. You are my shield and I trust in your daily word to me. I am filled with joy when I consider your loving kindness and my soul sings with happiness when I contemplate your wonderful deeds. You are my shepherd and my King. With you my life is protected like a fortress. Abide with me forever, O God. Amen.

25 FEBRUARY

The voice of Yahweh

PSALM 29

[1] Ascribe to Yahweh, you sons of God,
ascribe to Yahweh both glory and strength.
[2] Ascribe to Yahweh the glory his name deserves,
worship Yahweh in splendour of holiness.
[3] The voice of Yahweh is over the waters;
the thunder of the God of glory,
Yahweh thunders over mighty waters.
[4] Yahweh's voice is full of power,
the voice of Yahweh is majestic.
[5] The voice of Yahweh shatters cedars,
Yahweh breaks the cedars of Lebanon.
[6] He makes Lebanon skip like a calf,
Sirion like a wild ox calf.
[7] Yahweh's voice flashes forth the lightning,
[8] the voice of Yahweh shakes the desert,
Yahweh shakes the desert of Kadesh.
[9] Yahweh's voice makes oak trees twist
and strips the forests bare.
All cry "Glory!" in his Temple.
[10] Yahweh is enthroned above the flood,
Yahweh is enthroned as king forever.
[11] May Yahweh grant his people strength!
May Yahweh bless his people with peace!

Your glory is wonderful beyond my understanding, O Lord, and your holiness is mysterious beyond my comprehension. The oceans echo your power and majesty: the lightning and the thunderstorm are subject to your rule. The deserts and forests of the world shake at your command. I glorify your name and I praise the glory of your kingdom. From your almighty power, O God, grant me strength to go through each day and fill my heart with your peace. Amen.

26 FEBRUARY

Cries of joy come with the dawn

Psalm 30:1-5

[1] O Yahweh, I will exalt you,
for you have raised me up,
and have not let my foes gloat over me.
[2] O Yahweh, my God,
I called to you for help,
and you healed me.
[3] O Yahweh, you brought me back from the grave,
you saved my life as I sank in the pit.
[4] Sing to Yahweh, you faithful ones,
praise his holy name.
[5] His anger passes in a moment,
but his favour lasts a lifetime;
weeping may last through the night,
but cries of joy come with the dawn.

I praise you for your healing power, O Lord, and I thank you for your daily help and guidance. For your special support in my time of trouble I praise you with my whole heart. With all the faithful I glorify your holy name, and with all who have received your grace I sing with joy. I was afraid in the dark, O God, but you have brought me to a delightful dawn. Amen.

27 FEBRUARY

You turned my mourning into dancing

PSALM 30:6-12

[6] When I was wealthy I used to think,
"I can never be shaken!"
[7] O Yahweh, when you favoured me,
you made me as firm as a mountain;
and when you hid your face from me,
I was dismayed.
[8] I called to you, O Yahweh;
I cried to Yahweh for mercy:
[9] "What do you gain from my death,
by my falling into the pit?
Will the dust give praise to you?
Will it proclaim your faithfulness?"
[10] O Yahweh, hear and have mercy on me;
O Yahweh, be my help.
[11] You turned my mourning into dancing;
you changed my sackcloth
to garments of joy,
[12] that my heart might praise you
and never be silent;
O Yahweh my God,
I will praise you forever.

In my prosperity I was self-confident, O Lord, and I believed I would stand forever. But then I lost sight of you and my heart fell. I cried to you for help because I thought I would be shamed before the world. But my sadness was changed into contentment and my mournful dirge was turned into a joyous dance. O God, I will praise you forever, for my heart will not be silent. Amen.

28 FEBRUARY

Into your hands I commit my spirit

PSALM 31:1-8

[1] In you, O Yahweh, I have found refuge;
let me never be put to shame;
deliver me in your righteousness.
[2] Listen to me and make haste to my rescue;
be my fortified citadel,
a fortress to save me.
[3] As you are my rock and my rampart,
be true to your name
and lead me and guide me.
[4] Set me free from the net
they have spread out for me,
for you are my refuge.
[5] Into your hands I commit my spirit,
redeem me, O Yahweh,
the God of truth.
[6] I hate all who worship useless idols;
I trust in Yahweh.
[7] I will rejoice and be glad in your faithful love,
for you saw my affliction
and cared for me in my distress.
[8] You have not left me to the will of the enemy,
but have set me free
to go where I will.

You are my fortress and my rock, O Lord, and by your grace I shall be faithful and true. The net of temptation is ever before me, but you are my refuge. I commit myself into your hands this day and I hope for your redemption. Teach me not to worship riches and power, but to put my trust in you. Free me from all evil powers, O God, that I may live for ever in the warmth of your constant love. Amen.

1 MARCH

O Yahweh, show me mercy

PSALM 31:9-13

[9] O Yahweh, show me mercy, for I am in trouble,
sorrow weakens my eyes,
my soul and my body.
[10] My life fades with anguish, my years with groaning;
my strength fails through affliction
and my bones grow frail.
[11] My foes have made me the scorn of my neighbours;
my friends shrink away from me,
passers-by flee from me.
[12] People forget me as if I were dead,
I am like broken pottery.
[13] I hear many slanders; they cause terror around me,
conspiring against me,
to end my life.

Have mercy on me, O God, in my time of trouble. When life seems hopeless, grant me succour; when my strength fails, give me your grace; and when I am alone, show me your love. My spirit is broken and I am the scorn of my neighbours. I can only turn to you, for I know that you are the never failing fountain of life. Have pity on me, O God, in my weakness. Amen.

2 MARCH

My future is in your hand

PSALM 31:14-18

[14] But in you, O Yahweh, I put my trust,
and say, "You are my God."
[15] My future is in your hand;
save me from my foes
and from those who chase after me.
[16] Let your face shine on your servant
and save me in your faithful love.
[17] O Yahweh, I call to you, do not let me be shamed;
let shame be for the wicked,
let them sink into the grave.
[18] Silence their lying mouths,
and the arrogant contempt
they shout at the righteous.

I put my whole trust in you, O Lord, and I place my future in your hands. Although I am sometimes surrounded by people who mock at my faith, I know that you will vindicate me. Silence the contemptuous and save me from their evil ways. May your face shine on the righteous who trust in you and may their faith be unwavering. Into your hands, O God, I commend my soul, this day and always. Amen.

3 MARCH

How great is your goodness

Psalm 31:19-24

[19] How great is your goodness,
which you have stored up
for all who fear you;
you give it openly
to those who trust in you.
[20] Safely you hide them,
concealed by your presence
from human plotting;
you shield them in your home,
safe from the strife of tongues.
[21] Praise be to Yahweh,
who worked deeds of faithful love
when I was besieged.
[22] In my terror I cried,
"I am shut from your sight!"
but you heard my appeal
when I called for your help.
[23] Love Yahweh, all his faithful!
Yahweh protects the faithful,
but pays the arrogant in full.
[24] Be strong and take heart,
all you who hope in Yahweh.

Your goodness overwhelms me, O God, and I am filled with love for you. Hide me from all evil and shield me from all harm. I praise you for your constant love and for the times when you have answered my prayers. I pray that I may learn to love you and that I may remain faithful to my calling. My hope lies in you, O God, and my heart is strong when you are with me. Amen.

4 MARCH

You will save me from trouble

Psalm 32:1-7

[1] Blessed are those whose faults are forgiven,
whose sins are covered;
[2] they are blessed whom Yahweh says are guiltless,
whose spirit harbours no deceit.
[3] While I kept silent my body was wasting
because of my groaning
all the day long,
[4] for day and night your hand lay heavy,
and sapped my strength like summer heat.
[5] Then I admitted my sin to you
and did not hide my iniquity.
I said, "I will tell all my faults to Yahweh",
and you forgave my sinful guilt.
[6] Let all who are faithful turn to you
while you may be found;
when the mighty waters rise
they will never reach them.
[7] You are a place where I can hide,
you will save me from trouble
and surround me with salvation.

When I have sinned I feel I am estranged from you, O Lord, because you are holy and righteous and I am unworthy. But when I confess my sin to you, after much weariness and groaning, then I find my renewal in you.

Cover my sins with your loving forgiveness, O God, that I may turn to you again in trust and faith. You are my hiding place in times of trouble and there is no salvation except in you. Amen.

5 MARCH

Faithful love

PSALM 32:8-11

[8] I will teach you and show you
the way you should go;
I will advise you
and watch over you.
[9] Do not be like a horse or a mule
which cannot understand,
which need bit and bridle
or they will not obey.
[10] The wicked feel many pains,
but faithful love
enfolds all who trust Yahweh.
[11] Rejoice and be glad in Yahweh,
you righteous;
shout for joy,
all you honest of heart!

Teach me your ways, O Lord, and lead my footsteps on my pilgrimage through life. Save me from obstinacy and disobedience and give me the wisdom to avoid temptation. I know the pain that follows sin, but I seek instead the joy of repentance. I will rejoice and be glad in you, O God, for you have given me a true heart again. Amen.

6 MARCH

Yahweh loves righteousness and justice

PSALM 33:1-5

[1] Shout for joy to Yahweh, you righteous;
it is right for the upright to praise him.
[2] Praise Yahweh with harp;
play for him on the ten-stringed lyre.
[3] Sing him a new song,
play it with all your skill,
shout out with joy!
[4] For the word of Yahweh
is right and true;
he is faithful in all that he does.
[5] Yahweh loves righteousness and justice;
the earth is full of his faithful love.

My heart is glad when I see how the world is full of your love, O God. I praise you with my whole being and my every day is filled with the music of thanksgiving. Your word is wonderful to me, for it is always sure. May I be faithful also, Lord, in my words and deeds. As you love justice and righteousness, may I also love just dealing and right actions. Amen.

7 MARCH

Let all the earth be in awe of Yahweh

PSALM 33:6-12

[6] By the word of Yahweh the heavens were made,
the many stars by the breath of his mouth.

[7] He gathers the oceans into heaps
and stores the deep in his treasure-house.
[8] Let all the earth be in awe of Yahweh;
let all the world's peoples honour him,
[9] for the moment he spoke, it came to be,
he gave the command, and it all stood firm.
[10] Yahweh foils the plans of nations;
he frustrates the plots of peoples;
[11] but Yahweh's plans stand firm forever,
his heart's designs from age to age.
[12] That nation is blessed whose God is Yahweh,
the people he chose to be his own.

I praise you for the wondrous works of creation, O Lord. I praise you for your almighty word which spoke to the stars and the oceans in creation. The whole earth glorifies you and I worship you with my whole heart. Your word stands forever and no one can frustrate your plans. I pray that the nations may listen to your word and I ask your blessing upon those you have called to be your people. Amen.

8 MARCH

Yahweh it is who fashions all hearts

Psalm 33:13-22

[13] Yahweh looks down from heaven,
and all nations are in his sight;
[14] from his dwelling place he watches
all who live on earth.
[15] He it is who fashions all hearts,
and keeps a watch on all they do.

[16] No king is saved by his army's size,
nor can his strength save a warrior's life.
[17] No one can hope in a horse for safety;
despite its great strength it cannot save.
[18] But Yahweh's eyes are on those who fear him,
on those who trust in his faithful love
[19] to save them from death
and preserve them in famine.
[20] We are waiting for Yahweh,
our help and our shield,
[21] and our hearts rejoice in him,
for we trust his holy name.
[22] Yahweh, let your faithful love
rest on us,
as we have put our hope in you.

In your all-seeing wisdom, O Lord, I pray that you will watch over me and that you will draw my heart towards your love. No one will prosper without you beside him (or her) and even the powerful of this world are wholly in your hands. Bless those who wait upon you, O God, and shield those who need your help. I praise your holy name and give thanks for your faithful love. Amen.

9 MARCH

Taste and see that Yahweh is good

Psalm 34:1-10

[1] I will bless Yahweh at all times;
his praise will ever be on my lips.
[2] I will glory in Yahweh;
let the humble hear and rejoice.

[3] Proclaim the greatness of Yahweh with me,
let us exalt his name together.
[4] I looked for Yahweh and he answered me,
he saved me from all my fears.
[5] Those who look to him are radiant,
they never hang their heads in shame.
[6] Here is one who cried out in anguish;
Yahweh heard him
and saved him from all his troubles.
[7] The angel of Yahweh guards those who fear him
and rescues them.
[8] Taste and see that Yahweh is good;
how blessed are they
who take refuge in him!
[9] Fear Yahweh, you holy ones of his;
those who fear him lack no good thing.
[10] Young lions may grow weak and hungry,
but those who fear Yahweh
lack no good thing.

Every day I praise you, O Lord, and my heart lifts to your glory. May the whole earth glorify your name with me, for it is indeed wonderful! You have saved me from many dangers and from many temptations and your holy angels have watched over my path. Those who fear you need have no fear of others, because you are with those who seek your presence. May your providential care always be around my every footstep, O God. Amen.

10 MARCH

The fear of Yahweh

PSALM 34:11-17

[11] Come, my children, listen to me;
I will teach you the fear of Yahweh.
[12] If you relish your life,
and would live many days
with time to enjoy prosperity,
[13] guard your tongue from evil,
and your lips from deceit;
[14] turn from evil and do good;
look for peace and pursue it.
[15] The eyes of Yahweh are on the righteous,
and his ear is turned to their cry;
[16] but Yahweh sets his face against the wicked,
to blot out their memory from the earth.
[17] They cry out in anguish and Yahweh hears;
he rescues them from all their troubles.

Teach me your ways, O God, and walk with me throughout my days upon earth. May I depart from evil and may deceitfulness be far from me. I pray that I may follow peaceful paths under your watchful care and that my heart and mind may be set upon your righteousness. When I cry to you, O Lord, hear my prayer, and rescue me when I am in distress. Amen.

11 MARCH

Evil brings death to the wicked

PSALM 34:18-22

[18] Yahweh is close to the broken-hearted
 and saves those whose spirit is crushed.
[19] The upright may have many troubles,
 but Yahweh saves them from them all.
[20] Yahweh guards every bone in the body;
 not one of them is broken.
[21] But evil brings death to the wicked,
 the foes of the upright will be condemned.
[22] Yahweh ransoms the lives of his servants;
 none who take refuge in him are condemned.

Heal me when I am broken, O Lord, and search for me when I am lost. Guard me waking and sleeping, and prevent me from falling into error. I know that you will save those of upright heart, but that those who follow evil will not find eternal life. I pray that you will pay the ransom for me when I am the captive of temptation and that you will keep me safe in your house forever. Amen.

12 MARCH

I am your salvation

PSALM 35:1-8

[1] Withstand them, O Yahweh, who strive against me;
 fight against those who fight against me.
[2] Grasp shield and buckler;
 arise to my aid.

[3] Shake spear and javelin against my pursuers,
and say to my soul, "I am your salvation."
[4] Shame and disgrace on those out to kill me!
May those plotting against me
be repulsed in dismay.
[5] May they be chaff in the wind
with Yahweh's angel pursuing them;
[6] may their way be dark and slippery
with Yahweh's angel chasing them.
[7] Unprovoked they hid their net for me;
unprovoked they dug a trap for me.
[8] Unforeseen ruin overtakes them,
their own net entangles them,
they fall in their own pit to be destroyed.

Arise, O Lord, and pursue the armies of Satan. May your angels protect me from the many temptations which surround me. Be my shield each day and help me to repulse the powers of evil. Mischievous people set their cunning traps, but you, O God, entangle them in their own wicked devices. You are my salvation and in you I trust, now and forever. Amen.

13 MARCH

Yahweh rescues the poor

PSALM 35:9-18

[9] Then my soul shall delight in Yahweh,
and rejoice that he has saved me.
[10] My whole being will cry out,
"O Yahweh, who is like you,
who rescues the poor from those who oppress them,

the poor and the needy from those who rob
them?"

[11] Malicious witnesses come out against me
to ask me questions I cannot answer.

[12] They repay me evil for good,
lying in wait to make me forlorn.

[13] Yet when they were ill, I put on sackcloth and
humbled myself with fasting.
When my prayers went unanswered

[14] I went about mourning
as though for friend or brother,
with head bowed in grief
as if mourning my mother.

[15] But when I stumbled they thronged me in glee.
Unexpected attackers gathered against me;
they slandered unceasingly.

[16] If I slip they surround me,
grinding their teeth at me.

[17] How much longer, O Yahweh, will you just look
at them?
Rescue my life from those set to destroy me,
my precious life from lions.

[18] Then I shall praise you in the great assembly;
among crowds of people I shall give thanks
to you.

My soul delights in you, O Lord, for you have saved me. I pray that you will always be by my side when malicious people attack me or when slanderous accusations are made against me. Sometimes I feel that you are not listening to my prayer, but then you rescue me once again and my heart is full of joy. I wish to remain among the faithful always, and with them I will give thanks to you, O God, for all your love and care. Amen.

14 MARCH

O Yahweh, rise to my defence

Psalm 35:19-28

[19] Let no treacherous enemy gloat over me;
nor those who hate me without reason
leer at me spitefully.
[20] They do not speak peacefully,
but think up false charges
against peaceful people.
[21] They accuse me with shouting mouths:
"With our own eyes we saw it!"
[22] O Lord, you saw it, do not remain silent;
O Yahweh, stay near me;
[23] awake, and rise to my defence;
contend for me, my God and Lord.
[24] O Yahweh, my God,
judge me in your righteousness,
and do not allow them to gloat over me.
[25] Let them not think, "That is just what we wanted!"
Let them not say, "We have swallowed him up!"
[26] May all who gloat over my distress
be confused and dismayed,
covered with shame and disgrace;
all who exalt themselves.
[27] But let all who delight in my vindication
shout with joy and gladness;
let them always say, "All glory to Yahweh
who delights to see his servant prosper."

[28] My tongue shall speak of your saving justice,
and all day long I shall sing your praise.

Sometimes, O God, people behave spitefully and act falsely. I pray that such people may not prevail against the cause of justice. Speak for righteousness and goodness, Lord, and rise in the defence of the innocent. May your enemies be covered with shame and disgrace, but may all who wait for your love be blessed. I will sing your praises forever, for you are my Saviour. Amen.

15 MARCH

Your faithfulness reaches to the skies

PSALM 36:1-6

[1] Sin speaks to the wicked
deep within their hearts;
there is no fear of God
before their eyes.
[2] They flatter themselves
in their own sight
that their sin and hatred
cannot be exposed.
[3] The words of their mouths
speak lies and malice;
they have ceased to be wise
and do good.
[4] Even in bed they plot evil
and settle on a sinful plan;
there is no wickedness
too great for them.
[5] Your faithful love, O Yahweh,

reaches to the heavens;
your faithfulness
reaches to the skies.
[6] Your righteousness
is like a mountain range;
your judgements
are like the mighty deep.
You preserve, O Yahweh,
people and beasts.

Sin knows no boundaries in the hearts of the wicked, O God, and they pay no reverence to your glorious majesty. They hatch their evil plots and they produce lies and malicious gossip. Yet, you are the Lord of all and your righteousness is never failing. I rely upon you alone, O God, for you are faithful to the faithful and full of love to those who love. Amen.

16 MARCH

You are the fountain of life

PSALM 36:7-12

[7] How far beyond all price
is your faithful love;
all kinds of people
find refuge under your wings.
[8] They feast in your bountiful house;
you give them drink
from a river of delights.
[9] You are the fountain of life;
your light gives us light.
[10] Maintain your faithful love

to those who know you;
sustain your righteousness
to those whose heart is honest.
[11] Keep the foot of the proud
away from me;
stop wicked hands
from driving me away.
[12] See where the wicked lie fallen,
flung down and never to rise.

Your love is a pearl without price, O Lord, a refuge to those who seek it. In your light we can see the light of goodness, and your truth sustains the honest of heart. From you, all life springs like an everlasting fountain and to drink of it is a miracle of delight. Save me from pride and temptation, O God, and keep me safe from evil powers. Amen.

17 MARCH

Evil-doers will be destroyed

PSALM 37:1-9

[1] Do not get worried about the wicked,
or envy those who do wrong.
[2] They wither as quickly as grass,
they fade like the green of the fields.
[3] Trust in Yahweh, and do good;
you will dwell in the land
of safe pastures.
[4] Find your delight in Yahweh,
and he will give you
your heart's desire.

[5] Commit your way to Yahweh,
trust him and he will act;
[6] he will make your righteousness
as clear as the dawn,
and the justice of your cause
like the sun at noon.
[7] Be quiet before Yahweh
and patiently wait for him;
do not worry when people get their own way,
when their devious schemes
seem to succeed.
[8] Control your anger and turn from rage;
do not worry,
it only brings evil.
[9] Evil-doers will be destroyed;
those who hope in Yahweh
will be given the land.

I know, O Lord, that any triumph of evil will fade away quickly in the face of your righteousness. But my heart's desire is to stay with you forever, and to follow your delightful ways. I wait for you, O God, and I commit my whole life to you. I wait for the dawn of your goodness each day and my prayer is for the victory of the cause of justice. Hear my prayer, and let my cry come to you. Amen.

18 MARCH

The lives of the blameless are in Yahweh's care

PSALM 37:10-20

[10] In a little while the wicked will be finished;
though you look for them

they cannot be found.
[11] The meek will inherit the earth,
and enjoy boundless prosperity.
[12] The wicked plot against the upright,
gnashing their teeth at them;
[13] but Yahweh laughs at the wicked,
knowing their end is in sight.
[14] The wicked draw their swords
and bend their bows
to bring down the poor and needy.
[15] Their swords will pierce their own hearts
and their bows will be broken.
[16] The just are better with little
than the wicked are with wealth,
[17] for the power of the wicked
will be shattered,
but Yahweh upholds the just.
[18] The lives of the blameless
are in Yahweh's care;
their inheritance will last forever;
[19] in troubled times they will not wither,
in time of famine
they will have plenty.
[20] But death will come to the wicked;
Yahweh's foes will be meadow flowers
which vanish like smoke.

I pray, O Lord, for meekness of spirit, that I may come into the true inheritance of eternal life. At times the powers of wickedness seem to prevail, but I know that you will overturn the seats of unjust power, just as they overturn the hopes of the poor and needy. I am happy with what each day brings in your providence, O God, and I do not seek wealth or power. Rather do I seek the comfort of your word. Amen.

19 MARCH

The righteous repay generously

PSALM 37:21-26

[21] The wicked borrow and do not repay;
the righteous repay generously.
[22] Those blessed by Yahweh
inherit the land;
those he curses
will be cut off.
[23] Yahweh delights in the way of those
whose steps he made secure;
[24] if they stumble they will not fall,
for Yahweh holds their hands.
[25] I once was young and now am old;
I never saw the just abandoned
or their children begging bread.
[26] They are generous in lending freely;
their children will be blessed.

I know, O Lord, that the wicked are selfish, and that the righteous are generous in all things. I pray your blessing, that I may be free in the kingdom of heaven. Hold my hand when the path is rough; make my steps safe on my pilgrimage; and watch me lest I fall. As I grow old, O God, let me grow wise in your ways. Let me borrow from your store of grace that I may share your love with others. Amen.

20 MARCH

You will always live securely

PSALM 37:27-29

[27] Turn from evil and do good,
then you will always live securely;
[28] for Yahweh loves the righteous
and will not forsake
those faithful to him;
they will be safe forever,
but offspring of the wicked will die.
[29] The just will inherit the land
and dwell in it forever.

Help me, O Lord, to turn from evil and to embrace goodness, that I may always dwell safely in your house. I know that you will never abandon the righteous or leave the faithful in the hands of Satan. I pray that I may be just in all my ways, that I may inherit the kingdom of heaven when my course upon earth is done. Amen.

21 MARCH

Wait for Yahweh

PSALM 37:30-36

[30] Wisdom comes from the lips of the just;
what their tongues say is right.
[31] Their hearts contain the law of their God;
their feet will never slip.
[32] The wicked lie in wait for the just,
hoping to take their lives;

[33] but Yahweh will keep them from their power
and save them from death
when brought to trial.
[34] Wait for Yahweh and keep to his path;
he will exalt you to own the land
and you will see the wicked cut off.
[35] I have seen the wicked bring terror,
strong as a flourishing tree;
[36] when next I passed they were gone,
though I searched, they could not be found.

I seek wisdom in your eyes, O God, and I desire to do your will. Teach me your law of love and guide my every footstep. If evil powers plot to destroy the innocent, bring their plans to nought. When my ultimate trial comes, O God, I pray that you will defend my cause. This life is brief in your sight and I know that the enemies of good do not survive your final harvest. I pray, therefore, that your gracious goodness may abide with me through all the changes of my rented time on earth. Amen.

22 MARCH

Yahweh, refuge in time of trouble

PSALM 37:37-40

[37] Study the blameless and look at the just,
there is a future
for those who bring peace.
[38] But all the sinners will be destroyed;
the wicked's descendants
will be cut off.

[39] The just will have salvation from Yahweh;
he is their refuge in time of trouble.
[40] Yahweh helps them and rescues them;
he will save them from the wicked,
and keep them safe,
because they take refuge in him.

I pray for your peace in my heart, O Lord, that I may bring to the future and to those around me a little of the grace and love that I receive from you each day. May justice prevail in all my dealings and may my conscience be clear. Guide me away from the paths of wickedness and be my refuge in time of trouble. My salvation is in you, O God, and in you I trust. Amen.

23 MARCH

My iniquities a burden too heavy to bear

PSALM 38:1-8

[1] O Yahweh, do not rebuke me in your anger,
or discipline me in your wrath.
[2] For your arrows have pierced me,
and your hand has come down on me.
[3] Your wrath has left no health in my body,
and my bones have no health because of
my sin.
[4] My iniquities have poured over my head
like a burden too heavy to bear.
[5] My loathsome wounds fester
because of my folly.
[6] I am bowed down and prostrate;
I spend all day mourning.

[7] My loins burn with fever,
no part is unscathed.
[8] Numbed and utterly crushed,
I groan aloud in distress of heart.

Sometimes I behave very foolishly, O Lord, and the burden of my sin is difficult to bear. The arrows of conscience pierce me through and through and I am weighed down by my wrongdoings. It is as if I were in mourning and I long for the days of my innocence. How long, O God, must I suffer the wrath which I deserve? Have pity on me in my despair. Amen.

24 MARCH

You know all my longings, O Lord

PSALM 38:9-14

[9] You know all my longings, O Lord,
my sighing is not hidden from you.
[10] My heart is throbbing, my strength has failed;
the light has faded from my eyes.
[11] My friends and companions shun my wounds;
even my neighbours keep far away.
[12] Those who would harm me have set their traps;
those who want ill for me talk of my ruin;
all day long they plot their treachery.
[13] But I hear nothing, as if I were deaf;
I say not a word like someone dumb.
[14] I behave like one who does not hear,
whose mouth can offer no defence.

You know my deepest thoughts and desires, O Lord, and you know my loneliness and my desperation. The joy of living I once had is lost and my eyes are dim with my tears. Those around me seem to be against me and I imagine how they are plotting to bring about my downfall. I am bereft of speech and my ears are stopped. I have no defence but you, O God. Hear my voice, I beseech you. Amen.

25 MARCH

O Yahweh my God, do not desert me

PSALM 38:15-22

[15] In you, O Yahweh, I put my hope;
you, Lord my God, will make reply.
[16] I said, "Do not let them gloat over me,
or exalt over me when my foot slips."
[17] I am on the brink of falling,
and my pain is always with me.
[18] I do indeed confess my guilt,
I am troubled by the thought of my sin.
[19] I have many enemies, all without cause;
unprovoked, there are many who hate me,
[20] who repay my good with evil,
and slander me when I mean good.
[21] O Yahweh my God, do not desert me,
do not be far from me,
[22] be quick to help me,
O Lord my Saviour.

My hope lies entirely in you, Lord, and I pray that you will speak on my behalf. Although I am guilty of sin and am ready to fall over a cliff of agonising despair, yet I trust in you. Any good I do seems to come to nothing, and evil powers encompass me about. Grant me not what I deserve, O God, but let me hope instead for your compassionate love. Amen.

26 MARCH

The length of my life is as nothing before you

PSALM 39:1-6

[1] I said, "I will keep close watch on my ways,
so that what I say may be free from sin;
I will keep a muzzle on my mouth
as long as the wicked are present with me."
[2] I kept still silence, not even saying good,
but my anguish increased.
[3] My heart had smouldered within me
the fire flared up as I pondered,
and the words came bursting out:
[4] "O Yahweh, show me the end of my life,
how long I have to live,
how fleeting are my days.
[5] You have given me a mere handsbreadth of life,
the length of my life is as nothing before you,
each human life is only a breath.
[6] Each human being is only a shadow
which flits here and there but always in vain;
the heaped-up riches could go anywhere."

I try to keep a wise tongue in an evil world, O God, and I endeavour to avoid falling into sin. But sometimes I wonder why I have to be so constrained, and my anger at the futility of life comes to the surface. Life is so short compared with your eternity. I am like a shadowy moth flitting through the night and anything I have gained is like a useless heap of pebbles. I ask you, Lord, for true wisdom, for I am lost without your guidance. Amen.

27 MARCH

Lord, my hope is in you

PSALM 39:7-13

[7] So now, Lord, what am I seeking?
My hope is in you.
[8] Save me from all my transgressions;
make me no longer the butt of fools.
[9] I am silent, I would not open my mouth,
for you yourself have done all this.
[10] Take your scourge away from me;
I am overcome by the blows of your hand.
[11] You rebuke people by punishing sin;
like a moth you eat away all their wealth;
each person is only a breath.
[12] O Yahweh, hear my prayer;
listen to my cry for help;
do not close your ears to my weeping.
For I dwell with you as an alien,
a stranger, as all my fathers were.
[13] Turn from me, and I will look cheerful,
before I depart and cease to be.

All things come from you, O God, and so perhaps the whip that lashes me within is a punishment for all my transgressions. Yet I repent of my sins with many tears and pray that you will come to me, not with a scourge, but with your healing love. I am like an alien in a foreign land, a stranger to you, because of my shortcomings. Take away this burden of guilt, Lord, and smile upon my remaining days. Amen.

28 MARCH

Blessed are those who trust in Yahweh

PSALM 40:1-5

[1] I waited patiently for Yahweh;
he turned to me and heard my prayer.
[2] He pulled me out of the seething pit,
from the mud and mire,
and set my feet on rock,
to make my steps secure.
[3] He gave my mouth a new song,
a song of praise to our God.
Many will see with awe
and put their trust in God.
[4] Blessed are those who trust in Yahweh,
who do not turn to the proud,
to them that trust strange gods.
[5] How much you have done, O Yahweh my God,
in wonderful deeds and plans for us;
none can compare with you!
If I tried to speak and tell of them,
there would be too many to say.

I give you thanks, O Lord, for the times when you have saved me from slipping from the straight path into serious sin. I long to sing your praises and pray that many others will hear my words and will put their trust in you. Save me from alien evil powers, O God, and help me to fulfil the plan of life you have for me. My words are insufficient to tell of your wonderful deeds. I simply pray that you will lead me in your way. Amen.

29 MARCH

O Yahweh, come quickly and help me

PSALM 40:6-13

[6] You want no sacrifice or offering,
    but you gave me a willing ear;
you did not look for whole burnt offerings
    or sacrifice for sin.
[7] Then I said, "Here I am, I have come;
    my record is in the book;
[8] I want to do your will, O my God;
    your law is in my heart."
[9] I proclaim the righteous news
    in the thronged assembly,
I do not close my lips,
    as you know, O Yahweh.
[10] I do not keep your righteousness
    locked away in my heart;
I declare your faithful salvation,
I tell of your faithful love and truth,
    in the thronged assembly.
[11] O Yahweh, do not withhold
    your mercy from me;
may your faithful love and truth
    always protect me;
[12] for numberless troubles surround me,

my sins have overtaken me,
and I cannot see my way.
They are more than the hairs on my head,
and my courage fails me.
[13] Be pleased, O Yahweh, to save me;
O Yahweh, come quickly and help me.

Although my sins are without number, O Lord, I desire to do your will. As you have listened to my prayer, so may I declare your love and truth to any who will listen to me. Your past mercies are a cause for deep joy within me; and so I seek your continuing protection from all evil. Save me from myself, O God, and guard me in the face of temptation. Amen.

30 MARCH

May Yahweh think of me

Psalm 40:14-17

[14] Put to shame and confusion
all who seek my life;
repulse them in disgrace
who try to do me hurt.
[15] Let those who shout "Aha!" at me
be aghast with shame.
[16] But let all those who seek you
rejoice and be glad in you;
let them cry out eternally,
who love your salvation,
"Exaltation to Yahweh!"
[17] But I am poor and in need,
may Yahweh think of me.

You are my helper, my saviour,
O my God, do not delay.

May those who scorn my faith in you be brought to see the truth, O God, that they may repent of their evil and seek your mercy. I know well that those who search for you will be found by you, and that they will rejoice in your never failing love. And I, in my need and poverty of spirit, seek your saving help night and day. Glory be to you, O God, for your salvation is wonderful in my understanding. Amen.

31 MARCH

Blessed is he who cares for the weak

PSALM 41:1-3

[1] Blessed is he who cares for the weak;
Yahweh delivers him in time of trouble.
[2] Yahweh will guard him and preserve his life,
give him security in the land
and never leave him to the will of his foes.
[3] Yahweh will tend him when he is ill
and heal him on his bed of sickness.

I know your care and love, Lord, and I pray that I may have your grace to give care and love to those around me who are in need. When I have been ill you have comforted me; when I have flagged you have sustained me; and when I have been in trouble you have rescued me. Guard me throughout my life upon earth, O God, that I may know you more deeply in the world to come. Amen.

1 APRIL

You uphold me in my innocence

PSALM 41:4-13

[4] "O Yahweh," I said, "Have mercy on me;
heal me, for I have sinned against you."
[5] My foes can only speak malice of me:
"When will he die and his name disappear?"
[6] Whoever comes to visit me speaks hypocritically,
when they have left they spread slander
about me.
[7] All my foes conspire against me.
They impute the worst to me, and say:
[8] "A vile disease has gripped him;
he will never get up from the place where
he lies."
[9] Even my close friend, whom I trusted,
who shared my bread with me,
has lifted his heel at me.
[10] O Yahweh, take pity and heal me,
that I may repay them in full.
[11] I know you are pleased with me,
for my foe cannot triumph over me.
[12] You uphold me in my innocence
and keep me in your presence forever.
[13] Praise be to Yahweh, God of Israel,
forever and ever. Amen and Amen.

Sometimes, O Lord, I experience the malice and hypocrisy of others. If I am tempted to retaliate using the same evil ways, I pray you will hold my tongue in check that I may speak nothing but your love. Yet, it is hard, for the hurt is deep within me. Keep me in innocence, O God, and abide with me forever. I praise your name with my whole heart, because I have known your love. Amen.

2 APRIL

My soul thirsts for God

PSALM 42:1-5

[1] As deer long for running streams,
I long for you, my God.
[2] My soul thirsts for God,
the living God;
when can I go and meet with God?
[3] Day and night I drink my tears;
all day long I live with taunts:
"Where is your God?"
[4] I call to mind, with heart's distress,
how I marched with throngs
to the house of God
amidst exultant shouts of praise,
the happy noise of pilgrimage.
[5] Why so sad? Why groans of pain?
Still hope in God; still give him praise;
my Saviour God.

I long to be with you, O Lord, and I am thirsty for the living waters of eternal life. Instead I have only my own tears to drink because you seem far away from me. I remember wonderful days of worship and festival and I long for those joys to return. How can I convince others of your love, O God, when I am in this spiritual exile? But in my sadness I praise you, for my hope is in you. Amen.

3 APRIL

In my pain I think of you

PSALM 42:6-11

[6] Deep in my pain I think of you,
from Jordan, the Hermons,
and Mizar's heights.
[7] Deep calls to deep as your cataracts roar;
as your waves and your breakers
roll over me.
[8] All day, unceasingly, God pours his love on me;
all night I sing to the God of my life.
[9] I will ask God, my rock,
"Why have you gone from me?
Why must I mourn, oppressed by the enemy?"
[10] My bones are all crushed with the taunts of
my foes.
All day they ask me,
"Where is your God?"
[11] Why am I downcast? Why all this sighing?
Put hope in God!
For I shall yet praise him.
my Saviour, my God.

Your love is wider and deeper than the ocean, Lord, and I feel your unfathomable love surging through my soul. Despite my pain and mourning, I am still aware of your love for me. Although the enemies of the faith taunt me for my belief in you, O God, I know you are with me. I praise you with my whole heart and soul because I know your promises are sure. Amen.

4 APRIL

Send light and truth

PSALM 43

[1] Uphold my cause, O God, from a godless nation.
Save me from liars and unjust attacks.
[2] You are my strength, O God.
Why now desert me?
Why must I mourn, oppressed by the enemy?
[3] Send light and truth
to guide me and lead me
to your holy mountain,
the place where you dwell,
[4] to the altar of God, the God of my joy.
I praise you with harp,
O God, my God.
[5] Why am I downcast? Why all this sighing?
Put hope in God!
For I shall yet praise him,
my Saviour, my God.

Your are my strength in time of trouble, O God, and in the midst of disbelief I embrace the assurance of your faithfulness. Your light and truth are my companions on my pilgrimage to heaven, and with you beside me, the path is clear ahead. I praise you mightily, as I hear the music of your kingdom echoing down the years. You are my Saviour, Lord, and in you I trust. Amen.

5 APRIL

You deliver us from our foes

PSALM 44:1-7

[1] O God, we have heard for ourselves,
our ancestors have told us
what you did in their days,
in days long ago.
[2] With your hand you drove out nations
and settled our forefathers;
you laid waste the nations
and made our fathers flourish.
[3] It was not our fathers' swords that won them the land,
nor by their arm did they win the victory.
It was your right hand, your arm,
and the light of your face,
for you loved them.
[4] O God, you are my king
who decrees Jacob's victories;
[5] through you we conquer our foes,
in your name we trample our enemies.
[6] I do not trust in my bow,
it is not my sword that brings me the triumph.
[7] for you deliver us from our foes;
you put our enemies to shame.

I thank you, O God, for the powerful sword of the Spirit which is my defence when evil powers assail your kingdom. Your light shines down the generations through the darkness of sin and misunderstanding. You are my King and my shield against all arrows of doubt and misfortune, for my own strength is of no avail. You alone are my safeguard against evil. Amen.

6 APRIL

Our enemies have plundered us

PSALM 44:8-16

[8] Our boast is always of God,
and we will praise your name forever.
[9] But now you have abandoned and humbled us;
you no longer march out with our armies.
[10] You make us fall back before the foe,
and our enemies have plundered us.
[11] You gave us up to be slaughtered like sheep;
you have scattered us among the nations.
[12] You sold your people for a trifle
and made no profit from the sale.
[13] You have made us the taunt of our neighbours,
the scorn and derision of those all around us.
[14] You have made us a byword among the nations,
the peoples shake their heads at us.
[15] All day long my disgrace confronts me,
and my face is covered with shame
[16] at the sounds of taunts and abuse
from my foe, bent on revenge.

Sometimes, O Lord, it seems as if the powers of evil have prevailed. I am greatly troubled by the triumphant taunts of your enemies. Why have you allowed this to happen when your power is illimitable? Why are your faithful people under siege? Yet, I know you have not abandoned your loyal servants to defeat by the armies of Satan. Deliver them speedily, O God. Amen.

7 APRIL

God knows the secrets of the heart

Psalm 44:17-22

[17] All this has come on us
though we had not forgotten you
or been false to the covenant;
[18] our hearts never turned away
nor our feet strayed from your path.
[19] But you crushed us
and made us a land for the jackals,
and covered us in deepest darkness.
[20] If we had forgotten the name of our God
or lifted our hands to a foreign god,
[21] would not God have found it out,
for he knows the secrets of the heart?
[22] For your sake we face death daily;
we are set aside as sheep for slaughter.

I have tried to be faithful to your covenant, O Lord, and I remember you each day in my prayers. Yet, sometimes I am crushed by events beyond my control and the powers of evil hold sway. You know the innermost secrets of my heart, O God, and I am completely open before your searching gaze. Keep me from danger as I go through each day, and when the time of my death comes, be my shepherd and lead me to your fold. Amen.

8 APRIL

Redeem us for your faithful love

PSALM 44:23-26

[23] Awake, O Lord! Why do you sleep?
Rouse yourself! Do not leave us forever.
[24] Why do you hide your face,
forgetting our misery and oppression?
[25] For we sink to the ground,
we lie prone in the dust.
[26] Arise and come to our aid;
redeem us for your faithful love.

When you seem to hide your face from me, Lord, I am miserable and the days are long. It is as if I am lying in the dust of a hot day waiting for the cool of the evening. Arise, O God, and come to my aid: be awake to my troubled dreams. Redeem me from my sins and fill me with your constant love. Amen.

9 APRIL

You are the fairest of all men

PSALM 45:1-5

[1] My heart is moved by a noble theme:
as I sing my song to the king
my tongue is the pen of a skilful scribe.
[2] You are the fairest of all men;
grace has been poured upon your lips,
for God has blessed you forever.
[3] Fasten your sword upon your thigh,

O mighty one;
advance in pomp and majesty.
[4] In majesty ride out as victor,
in the cause of truth,
humility and justice.
Do awesome deeds by your mighty power.
[5] Your arrows are sharp
in the the heart of royal foes;
nations fall beneath you.

You are King of the nations, O Lord, and you rule over the whole of heaven and earth. My pen could never do justice to your glory because you are so far beyond my comprehension. Your grace falls upon me like the soft rain of spring and the truth of your ways is like the summer sun before me. May I walk in humility, and may my dealings be just, in the little kingdom you have given to me in my own life. Amen.

10 APRIL

You love the just and hate the evil

Psalm 45:6-17

[6] God has enthroned you forever and ever,
your royal sceptre
is a sceptre of justice.
[7] You love the just and hate the evil,
so God, your God, has anointed you
with oil of joy above your fellows.
[8] Your robes are filled with fragrance:
myrrh, aloes and cassia.

Harps sound from ivory palaces
to make you glad.

[9] King's daughters are your ladies of honour;
at your right hand the queen
wears gold of Ophir.

[10] My daughter, listen to my words,
and think about them:
forget your people
and your father's house.

[11] The king is enthralled by your beauty;
bow down to him,
for he is your lord.

[12] The people of Tyre will court you with gifts;
the richest of people
will seek your favour.

[13] The princess is glorious within her chamber;
gold is woven in her gown.

[14] In splendid robes she is led to the king;
her companion virgins
will be brought to you.

[15] With joy and gladness
they come in procession
to enter the palace of the king.

[16] Instead of your fathers you shall have sons,
for you to make princes
in all the earth.

[17] I will pass your memory to all generations,
so that nations will praise you
forever and ever.

O Lord, you have filled the universe with beauty and riches beyond compare, and I pray that all your children may share in your bounty. Each person is a prince or princess in your eyes, O God, and I praise you for the wonderful gifts you have given to everyone, including myself. I pray that the marriage of earth to heaven may come soon; and may joy and gladness be in every heart when the splendid storehouse of your kingdom is perceived. Amen.

11 APRIL

God is our refuge and strength

PSALM 46:1-3

[1] God is our refuge and strength,
a timely help in trouble.
[2] Therefore we will not fear,
though the earth shakes and the mountains fall
into the depths of the sea;
[3] when the waters roar and foam
and the mountains quake and heave.

Be my refuge, Lord, when troubles come: be my strength in hours of weakness. If you are with me, nothing can make me afraid: if you are my help, then what should I fear? The mountains may tremble or the oceans may be thrown into turmoil, but the foundations of heaven are sure and will not fall. Be my refuge and strength forever, O God, and never forsake me, in life or in death. Amen.

12 APRIL

The holy place where the Most High lives

PSALM 46:4-7

[4] There is a river
whose streams bring joy to God's city,
the holy place where the Most High lives.
[5] God is within her, she cannot fall;
God will help her at break of day.
[6] Nations are in uproar,
kingdoms are falling;
he lifts his voice
and the earth melts.
[7] Yahweh of Hosts is with us.
The God of Jacob is our fortress.

I am full of joy, O Lord, when I drink of the water of life which flows from your heavenly city into my heart. The life of heaven is never-ending and it is wonderful to me to think that I may drink of that eternal life during my time upon earth. The world may be falling apart, yet I know your are with me. O God, be my fortress always. Amen.

13 APRIL

Come and see the wonders of Yahweh

PSALM 46:8-11

[8] Come and see the wonders of Yahweh,
the astonishing deeds
he has done on earth.

[9] He ends all wars throughout the earth;
he breaks the bow,
snaps the spear,
burns shields in the fire.
[10] "Be still, and know that I am God.
I am high over nations,
high over earth."
[11] Yahweh Almighty is with us.
The God of Jacob is our fortress.

I thank you, O Lord, for all the marvellous deeds you have done for humankind and for all the wonders of creation. I pray for the time when all wars will cease at your command. Fill my heart with the stillness of your eternal presence and bring peace to my soul. You are my refuge and my shelter in time of trouble, O God, and you are never far away. Amen.

14 APRIL

How awesome is Yahweh Most High

PSALM 47:1-4

[1] Clap your hands, all nations;
shout to God with songs of joy.
[2] How awesome is Yahweh Most High,
the great King of all the earth!
[3] He subdued nations under us,
put peoples under our feet.
[4] He chose our birthright for us,
the pride of Jacob whom he loves.

O King of the universe and Lord of heaven, I rejoice in the many signs of your presence in the world. Your holiness and power are wonderful to contemplate; and yet your love is deep within me. All nations and races are your offspring and each person's birthright is to be a child in your kingdom. I thank you for the marvel of your love for me, O God, and I pray for the grace to love my neighbour. Amen.

15 APRIL

God is king of all the earth

PSALM 47:5-9

[5] God has gone up with a shout of triumph,
Yahweh amid the trumpet sounds.
[6] Sing praise to God, sing praises!
Sing praise to our King, sing praises!
[7] For God is king of all the earth;
sing praises with a song!
[8] God reigns over the nations,
seated on his holy throne.
[9] The nations' nobles gather
as people of the God of Abraham,
for the mighty of earth belong to God,
and he is exalted on high!

Your glory is revealed in the clouds of heaven, O Lord, and the wonders of creation are heralds of your coming. I will sing your praise with all my heart from now until your kingdom dawns. Your rule is universal, O God, and all nations are your subjects. The rich and the mighty, along with the poor and the meek, will bow their heads before you, and your justice will prevail. My God, I praise you. Amen.

16 APRIL

God is Zion's stronghold

PSALM 48:1-8

[1] Great is Yahweh
 and most worthy of praise
in the city of our God,
 the holy hill.
[2] Beautiful and lofty,
 the joy of all the earth,
is Zion, mountain of the north,
 the Great King's city.
[3] God, in her palaces,
 has shown he is her stronghold.
[4] The alliance of kings
 advanced in force;
[5] they looked and were astounded;
 they fled in panic.
[6] Trembling seized them
 like women in labour.
[7] Like ships of Tarshish
 in the east wind, you wrecked them.
[8] What we had heard,
 we saw for ourselves
in the city of God,
 of Yahweh of Hosts,
which God makes secure forever.

I pray, O Lord, that the beauty of your heavenly city may be reflected in the growing vision of your kingdom upon earth. No praise is worthy of your holiness, but I ask that the joy which fills my heart may be acceptable as my prayer to you. All earthly powers tremble before your majesty, and your revelations shake the palaces of worldly kings. Your refuge in glorious Zion is my inspiration, O God, and I pray that this vision will never leave me. Amen.

17 APRIL

Our eternal God, our guide forever

PSALM 48:9-14

[9] O God, within your Temple
we reflect on your faithful love.
[10] Your name and praise, O God,
reach through all the world;
your power is full of justice.
[11] Mount Zion is glad,
Judah's daughters rejoice,
because of your judgements.
[12] Walk through Zion,
go right round her,
and count her towers,
[13] admire her ramparts,
and look at her palaces.
Tell future generations,
[14] that such is God,
our eternal God,
our guide forever.

Your constant love is marvellous for me to consider, Lord, and I praise you wholeheartedly for the strength you have given to those faithful to your word. Your kingdom is like a fortress all around me and its citadels stand as my defence against evil. I pray that your kingdom may fully come, so that the children of the future will know of your majesty and glory. Stay beside me forever, O God. Amen.

18 APRIL

No one can ever redeem himself

PSALM 49:1-9

[1] Hear this, all you nations,
listen, all the world's peoples,
[2] low and high, rich and poor:
[3] My lips have wisdom to speak,
my thoughts grant understanding;
[4] I will listen to a proverb,
and interpret my mystery
to the sound of the harp.
[5] Why should I fear troubled times,
when evil liars surround me,
[6] trusting their wealth
and boasting of opulence?
[7] No one can ever redeem himself
or pay God the cost of release.
[8] The redemption of a life
would be beyond your means
[9] if you lived forever
and never grew old.

Give me the wisdom to know how to teach others the truths of your kingdom, Lord. Those steeped in worldly ways have no real power, so why should I be afraid of human influence when all power is in your hands? You are the source of all life and even the longest human life is beyond redemption, except through you. I thank you, O God, that you have shepherded me into your fold and may I remain there forever. Amen.

19 APRIL

Even the mighty are not immortal

PSALM 49:10-14

[10] Everyone knows that the wise die
like the stupid and senseless,
and leave their wealth to others.
[11] Their tombs will be their dwellings forever,
their homes for countless generations,
even if countries bear their name.
[12] Even the mighty are not immortal
but become like the beasts that die.
[13] This end awaits all who trust in themselves,
and their disciples
who hang on their words.
[14] Like sheep they descend to the grave,
to be a meal for death;
in the morning the just
will rule over them.
All trace of their pomp will be gone,
and the grave will be their home.

The wise and the foolish come to the same end, O Lord, and each one enters through the gate of death. Their wealth is left for others to spend and their home in the tomb is forever. No human is immortal and those who trust only in themselves have little hope. The road to self-glory ends in the unmarked grave and great affairs wither on the branch. Only in you, Lord, do I trust, for in you is the fountain of eternal life. Amen.

20 APRIL

God will take me up

Psalm 49:15-20

[15] But God will ransom my soul;
he will take me up
from the clutch of the grave.
[16] Do not be impressed when people get rich
and live in ever greater pomp;
[17] they take nothing with them when they die,
their splendour does not follow them.
[18] While they lived
they thought they were blessed
(for people praise you
when you prosper),
[19] but they go to join their ancestors
and will never again
see the light.
[20] One who is rich without wisdom
is like the beasts who die.

I commend my soul into your hands, O God, for only you can pay the ransom of my death. The rich cannot take their wealth beyond the grave and their prosperity is of no account. The light of the sun shines no more upon them when they go the way of their ancestors. I pray, therefore, for wisdom to live my short life in your light, O God, for your light shines forever within my soul. Amen.

21 APRIL

God himself is judge

Psalm 50:1-6

[1] Yahweh God, the Mighty One, has spoken,
and summoned the world
from sunrise to sunset.
[2] God shines forth from Zion,
the perfection of beauty.
[3] Our God comes and will not be silent;
a fire devours ahead of him,
a storm rages around him.
[4] He summons the heavens above,
and the earth below to judgement.
[5] "Gather my faithful to me,
who sealed my covenant by sacrifice."
[6] The heavens declare his justice,
for God himself is judge.

Your light shines from heaven, Lord, and the whole world can see your glory. The beauty of your holiness is awesome to behold and your illimitable power is like a devouring fire to cleanse and renew. I pray for your guidance until that day when I am called to judgement, and when that day comes, O God, I rely upon your steadfast covenant with the faithful, for I have no strength in myself to survive the truth of your judgements. Abide with me, now and always. Amen.

22 APRIL

Make thanksgiving your offering to God

PSALM 50:7-15

[7] "Listen, my people, as I speak;
    Israel, hear the charges against you,
    for I am God, your God.
[8] I do not find fault with your sacrifices,
    your burnt offerings are always before me.
[9] I do not need a bull from your stall,
    or goats from your pens,
[10] for every beast in the wild is mine,
    and cattle on a thousand hills.
[11] I know every bird in the hills,
    and I own all that moves in the fields.
[12] If I were hungry I would not tell you,
    for I own the world and everything in it.
[13] Do I eat bulls' flesh or drink goats' blood?
[14] Make thanksgiving your offering to God;
    keep your vows to God Most High;
[15] then call to me in troubled days.
    I will save you, and you will honour me."

I know that my worship is inadequate, Lord, for your majesty in heaven is unimaginable, and yet at the same time, you rule over the whole universe you have created. You do not need me, but you have chosen me to do your work in the world in a very small way. I give you thanks for all your good gifts and I pray for the grace to be faithful to my calling. When my need is great, O God, I shall always call to you, for I know you are my salvation. Amen.

23 APRIL

I said nothing at all as you did all this

PSALM 50:16-23

[16] God says this to the wicked:
"What right have you to mouth my laws
or take my covenant on your lips?
[17] You detest my teaching,
and thrust my words behind you.
[18] You go to assist a thief you see,
you join in with adulterers;
[19] you use your mouth for evil,
and your tongue for speaking lies;
[20] you continually slander your brother
and malign your own mother's son.
[21] I said nothing at all as you did all this,
so you thought I was just like you,
but I charge and rebuke you to your face.
[22] Think about that, you who ignore God,
lest I rend you apart
with no one to save you.
[23] I am honoured by those who offer me thanks;
to those who follow my way
I will show God's salvation."

Teach me your wisdom, O God, that I may learn to keep your covenant, not only with my lips, but with my whole heart. Guard me from evil, and guide my every speech and action. Save me from hypocrisy and give me a lively conscience, that I may walk uprightly on my daily pilgrimage. Do not judge me according to my works, but according to your loving mercy upon the penitent. I thank you, Lord, for all your wonderful gifts. Amen.

24 APRIL

Have mercy on me, O God

PSALM 51:1-6

[1] Have mercy on me, O God, in your faithful love;
in your great compassion
blot out my offences.
[2] Wash away all my misdeeds,
and cleanse me from my sin.
[3] For I know my transgressions,
and my sin is always in mind.
[4] I have sinned against you, only you,
and done what you see to be wrong;
you are justified in your sentence
and blameless in your judgement.
[5] I have surely sinned from birth,
a sinner from my conception,
[6] but you want truth in the inner being,
so put your wisdom in my secret heart.

My sins are ever before me, O Lord, and I pray that the abundance of your compassion and your faithful love may descend upon me and wash away my misdeeds. Every sin is a sin against you and your holiness, and so I know the hurt I have caused you. I am aware of my ever ready tendency to sin, but you O God, can transform the human heart with your cleansing power. So may you do to me when I am truly penitent. Amen.

25 APRIL

Give me back the joy of salvation

Psalm 51:7-13

[7] Cleanse me with hyssop until I am clean;
wash me, that I may be whiter than snow.
[8] Let me hear joy and gladness,
let the bones you have broken rejoice.
[9] Turn your face from my sins,
and blot out all my misdeeds.
[10] Create a pure heart in me, O God;
renew a resolute spirit in me.
[11] Do not thrust me from your presence;
do not remove your spirit of holiness.
[12] Give me back the joy of salvation;
sustain me with a willing spirit.
[13] Then I will teach transgressors your ways,
and sinners will come back to you.

Cleanse me from my sin, O God, and renew my spirit. Let me rejoice in my brokenness, for now your healing power may refresh my innermost thoughts. May I stay always in your presence, inspired by your spirit of holiness; and may the joy of salvation flood through my whole being. Empower me, O Lord, to impart your gifts to others, that they also may know your loving care. Amen.

26 APRIL

My offering, O God, is a broken spirit

PSALM 51:14-19

[14] Save me from guilt of bloodshed,
O God, God of my salvation,
and my tongue will sing of your saving power.
[15] Open my lips, O Yahweh,
and my mouth will proclaim your praise.
[16] Sacrifice gives you no pleasure,
you do not desire burnt offerings.
[17] My offering, O God, is a broken spirit,
a broken and contrite heart
you will never scorn.
[18] In your good pleasure make Zion prosper,
and rebuild the walls of Jerusalem,
[19] so that you can delight in appropriate offerings,
burnt offerings and whole oblations,
then bulls will be sacrificed on your altar.

What sacrifice can I present to you, O Lord? Surely there is nothing worthy that I can give to you. Yet, I offer my broken spirit and my truly penitent heart, in the sure knowledge that you will not turn your face away from me. May your kingdom come upon earth, as it already is in heaven, and may the vision of the true Jerusalem fill my thoughts as I journey towards the gateways of your heavenly city. Amen.

27 APRIL

Why are you so proud of being wicked?

PSALM 52:1-7

[1] Why are you so proud of being wicked,
you man of might?
Why do you spend all day boasting,
of evil against the godly?
[2] You plan destruction;
your tongue is sharp as a razor,
plotting deceitful deeds.
[3] You love evil more than good,
and lying more than truth;
[4] you love using harmful words,
with devious tongue.
[5] Therefore God will crush you forever,
snatch and tear you from your tent,
uproot you from among the living.
[6] The just will watch it with awe.
They will mock him and say,
[7] "Here is the man who spurned God as his
stronghold,
but trusted his opulence
and his power to destroy!"

I seek richness of spirit, Lord, not the wealth that worldly people store in vain. I seek humility in your service, not the pride that goes with ambition or self-glory. Teach me goodness and truth and help me to cast aside evil and falsehood. May evil powers receive the judgement they deserve. I pray, O God, for your bountiful grace that I may find in your holiness the deep fulfilment of my soul. Amen.

28 APRIL

In God's eternal faithful love I trust

PSALM 52:8-9

[8] But I am like an olive tree
growing in the house of God;
in God's eternal faithful love
I put my trust.
[9] I will praise you forever for what you have done,
I will trust in your name,
for it is good,
in the presence of the faithful.

Anoint me with the oil of your faithful love, O God, that I may grow in your ways like an olive tree in fertile earth. I trust in you as a child trusts his (her) parents, for I know that your constancy will never falter. May I be constant in my faith, and may I honour your name in my thoughts, in my deeds and in my words, this day and always. Amen.

29 APRIL

Not one of them does right

PSALM 53:1-3

[1] The fool has said in his heart,
"There is no God."
They are depraved and their deeds are vile;
not one of them does any good.
[2] God looks down from heaven
on all the human race

to see if any are wise,
if any seek after God.

[3] All have turned away,
they have all become corrupt,
not one of them does right,
not even one.

Teach me your wisdom, Lord, for I am but a child in the face of the powers of evil. Folly surrounds me and temptation is strong. You know me through and through, and only you can guide me to the end of this labyrinth of dangerous pathways. May those who have rejected you see the light of your truth. Hear my prayer, O God, and abide with me forever. Amen.

30 APRIL

They will be gripped in terror

PSALM 53:4-6

[4] Will the evil never learn,
they who devour my people as bread,
and never call to God?

[5] They will be gripped in terror,
even when there is no need for fear.
God scatters your attackers' bones;
you shamed them,
for God despised them.

[6] O that Israel's salvation
would come from Zion!
When God restores his people's fortunes,
let Jacob rejoice
and Israel be glad.

It is hard for me to learn the ways of goodness, O God, for the powers of Satan beguile me constantly. But when I fall I am afraid, for you then seem far away. Scatter the dark shadows of temptation and lift my head again. My salvation comes from your heavenly city and only you, O Lord, will restore me to the riches of your grace. Amen.

1 MAY

Yahweh, mainstay of my life

PSALM 54

[1] Save me, O God, by your name;
set me free by your might.
[2] Listen, O God, to my prayer;
hear me as I speak to you.
[3] The violent are attacking me;
pitiless people seek my life.
They give no thought to God.
[4] Surely, my defence is God:
Yahweh, mainstay of my life.
[5] May those who wait to ambush me
see their own evil strike them down.
[6] I will freely sacrifice
to praise you, O Yahweh,
as is right.
[7] For he has saved me from all troubles.
I watch with delight as my enemies fall.

Your name is wonderful in my prayer, O Lord, for to call upon you is to seek the freedom of your love. All around me people are cruel to each other and they give little thought to you. Be my strength in the face of evil, and grant me your peace deep within my heart. I praise you mightily, for you have saved me in time of trouble. O God, walk before me always. Amen.

2 MAY

Hear my prayer, O God

PSALM 55:1-11

[1] Hear my prayer, O God,
do not ignore my plea.
[2] Hear me and answer me,
my cares leave me no peace.
[3] I am quaking at the hostile shouts,
at the clamour of the wicked,
who heap up trouble against me
and revile me in their fury.
[4] My heart is torn with anguish;
the terrors of death attack me.
[5] Fear and trembling beset me;
horror has overwhelmed me.
[6] I cry for the wings of a dove
to fly away and be at peace,
[7] to escape far away and be safe in the desert.
[8] I would soon find myself a nest,
far from the deluge and storm.
[9] Confuse the wicked, O Lord,
frustrate their plotting,
I see riot and strife in the city.
[10] Day and night they prowl round its walls;
rumour and scandal are in it.
[11] Destructive forces roam free in the city;
threats and lies never leave its streets.

I am under constant pressure, Lord, from those around me. At times I am full of despair because the wicked seem to prevail. I am so frightened when the forces of evil encircle me that I wish I had wings to fly away. I pray that you will frustrate the plots of lawless people in the cities that Satan tries to build. Hear my prayer, O God, and fill me with your peace. Amen.

3 MAY

I cry out in distress

PSALM 55:12-21

12 If a foe was insulting me,
I could endure it;
if a foe rose against me,
I could avoid him.
13 But it is you, my equal
who shared my bread, my closest friend,
14 whom I once joined in fellowship
as we walked with the crowd in the house of God.
15 Let death take my enemies unawares;
let them go to the grave alive,
for evil shares their home with them.
16 But I call to God,
and Yahweh will save me.
17 At dusk, dawn and noon
I cry out in distress,
and he listens to me.
18 He ransoms me and gives me peace
from the strife against me,
though many oppose me.
19 God, enthroned in eternity,
will hear them and strike them,
who never change, never fear God.
20 Such a person strikes his friends,
violates his covenant;

[21] with a mouth as smooth as butter,
but a heart that harbours war;
with words that seem smoother than oil,
yet they cut like drawn swords.

Who can I trust but you, Lord? Enemies attack me and even friends let me down. Only you will pay my ransom to release me from the conflicts that are bred by hate. Give me your grace, O God, that I may keep my word, that I may be loyal to friends in trouble, that I may keep the covenant of faith. I place my soul in your care, this day and always. Amen.

4 MAY

I trust in you

PSALM 55:22-23

[22] On Yahweh cast your cares;
he will sustain you.
He never lets the righteous fall.
[23] You, O God, will thrust down the wicked
into corruption's pit;
thirsty for blood and devious,
they will not live half their days.
But I trust in you.

All my cares and troubles I place in your hands, O God, for I know that you will help those who appeal to your compassion and love. All wicked deeds will be punished by your justice, but those who seek righteousness will be held up by the strength you give. Keep me from corruption's snares, Lord, and guide my footsteps each day. In you I put my trust. Amen.

5 MAY

What can mortals do to me?

PSALM 56:1-9

[1] Take pity on me, O God, for they harry me;
all day long they press their attack.
[2] My slanderers beset me throughout the day;
many are fighting me from the heights.
[3] When I am afraid I trust in you,
[4] in God, whose word I praise.
In God I trust and I will not be afraid.
What can mortals do to me?
[5] All day long they twist my words;
all their plans are aimed at me.
[6] They plot in their malice and watch for me,
determined to take my life.
[7] Reject them, O God, because of this crime;
in your fury bring down the nations.
[8] You have noted my grief; list my tears in your book;
are they not in your records?
[9] Then my foes will retreat when I call for help.
This I know, that God is on my side.

Help me to avoid those who stir up trouble, Lord. If you are with me, I am not afraid of what anyone can do to me: malice and slanders will not touch me. I know that you have recorded my tears of despair and I trust you with my body and soul, because you are my Creator and Sustainer. I also know that you have recorded good and evil deeds and that your judgement is certain. If you are on my side, Lord, who can prevail over me? Amen.

6 MAY

For you have delivered my soul from death

PSALM 56:10-13

[10] In God, whose word I praise,
in Yahweh, whose word I praise,
[11] in God whom I trust, I will not be afraid.
What can a human do to me?
[12] I have made my vows to you, O God;
I will fulfil them with sacrifices.
[13] For you have delivered my soul from death,
my feet from slipping,
to walk before God in the light of life.

I praise the gift of your holy word, O Lord, and I rejoice in your covenant of love. I have vowed to follow your word all the days of my life and I ask for the grace to fulfil my promises. When you are with me I am not afraid of what any human being can do to me, because your grace is sufficient for my needs. To walk with you, O God, is to walk in the light of eternal life where death has no power over me. Amen.

7 MAY

In you, O God, my soul takes refuge

PSALM 57:1-6

[1] O God, be gracious to me, be gracious,
for in you my soul takes refuge.
I seek refuge in the shadow of your wings
until the disaster has passed.

[2] I call to God Most High,
to God who will work his purpose in me.
[3] He sends from heaven to save me,
repulses those who harry me;
May God send his love, faithful and sure.
[4] I lie in the midst of man-eating lions
with spears and arrows for teeth,
and sharp swords for tongues.
[5] Be exalted above the heavens, O God,
your glory above all the earth!
[6] They spread a net for my feet,
I was bowed down with care.
They dug a pit in my path
but fell into it themselves.

I pray, O Lord, that your purpose will so work in me that I shall be a fit vessel for your grace. Despite the powers of evil which set their cunning traps and nets for me, I trust in your providence. Hide me under the shadow of your wings when I am afraid and keep my soul forever in your secure refuge. Save me from the lions of Satan and fill me with your constant love. I glorify your name with all my heart, O God! Amen.

8 MAY

Your faithful love is as high as the heavens

PSALM 57:7-11

[7] My heart is ready, O God, my heart is ready;
I will sing and make music for you.
[8] Wake up, my soul! Wake up, lyre and harp,
that I may awake the dawn!

[9] I will praise you among the peoples, O Yahweh,
and play music to you among nations,
[10] for your faithful love is as high as the heavens;
your faithfulness reaches the sky.
[11] Be exalted above the sky, O God,
your glory above all the earth!

My heart is full of praise for you, my God! My soul could sing forever of your faithful and constant love: I could make the music of your glory from now until the day I die, and then to eternity. Your love is greater than the universe, greater than all the courts of heaven. All the nations of the world will sing your praise, for your glory is manifest in your creation. I praise you, O God! My God, I praise you! Amen.

9 MAY

You rulers, do you indeed rule justly?

PSALM 58

[1] You rulers, do you indeed rule justly?
Do you judge fairly the people of earth?
[2] No, in your hearts you devise injustice;
you use your power to deal out violence.
[3] The wicked have gone astray from the womb,
from the day of their birth they stray and lie.
[4] Their poison is like the venom of snakes,
like the deaf adder that blocks its ears
[5] to avoid the sound of the charmers' tune,
no matter how skilfully they play.
[6] O God, break their teeth in their mouths;
snap these young lions' fangs, O Yahweh.

[7] Make them vanish like draining water;
make them wither like trampled grass,
[8] like a slug that dissolves as it moves,
or a stillborn child that never sees light.
[9] As quickly as fire of thorns heats pots,
whether green or dry,
may retribution sweep them away.
[10] The just will rejoice to see vengeance done,
when they wash their feet
in the blood of the wicked.
[11] Then all will say that the just are rewarded;
there is a God who gives justice on earth.

The rulers of this world are powerful, but in their power their corruption may take root. I pray, O Lord, that you will give wisdom to those who have positions of power; I pray that justice will prevail for both rich and poor; and I pray that the wicked may receive the retribution they deserve. May the just rule of your kingdom be supreme throughout the world. Hear my prayer, O Lord. Amen.

10 MAY

Rescue me from evil-doers

PSALM 59:1-8

[1] Deliver me from my foes, O God;
be my strong tower against those who attack me.
[2] Rescue me from evil-doers
and save me from all who thirst for blood.
[3] See how they lie in wait for me!
The violent plot to ambush me,

for no sin or fault of mine, O Yahweh.
[4] Though I did no wrong, they rush to attack me.
Rise up to help me; see my plight!
[5] O Yahweh, God of Hosts, God of Israel,
rise up to punish all the nations;
show no mercy to wicked traitors.
[6] They come at nightfall, snarling like dogs,
prowling the city.
[7] See what they mouth, spew swords from their lips,
and say, "Who can hear us?"
[8] But, O Yahweh, you laugh at them,
you scoff at all nations.

Deliver me from all evil powers, Lord, and strengthen me against all temptation. Unsuspected, wickedness seems to grow until it takes over the seat of earthly power. Rise up, and send your heavenly power to change our world and charge it with goodness and love. The might of the wicked is nothing to you, O God, and so, may your Spirit stir the souls of the faithful to struggle for justice and peace. Amen.

11 MAY

The God who loves me will go on before me

PSALM 59:9-15

[9] I keep watch for you, my strength,
you are my strong tower, O God.
[10] The God who loves me faithfully
will go on before me
and let me gloat over the foes who beset me.
[11] Do not destroy them, O Lord our shield,

lest my people forget;
in your might make them scatter
and bring them to ruin.

[12] For the sins of their mouths and the words of their lips,
make them trapped in their pride,
for their curses and lies.

[13] Consume them in anger, consume them to the end.
Then the whole earth will know
that God rules in Jacob.

[14] They come back at nightfall,
snarling like dogs,
and prowling the city.

[15] They scavenge for food
and howl if unsatisfied.

You are my strength and shield, O God, and in you I find my refuge. Your rule is over the whole universe and no wickedness or sin can survive in the face of your will. Defeat all pride and falsehood and scatter the forces of evil to the four winds. May your love be victorious within me, O God, and throughout the world. Walk before me and make me whole. Amen.

12 MAY

I will sing of your love

PSALM 59:16-17

[16] But I will sing of your strength,
of your love in the morning;
for you are my strong tower,
my refuge in trouble.

[17] O my Strength, I sing praise to you;
you, O God, are my strong tower;
faithful in love for me.

I will praise you in the morning and I will praise you in the evening, O God, for you are my strength and my unassailable tower. Who else but you can defend me in all the chances and changes of this life? Who but you can be my defence against the powers of evil? May my love be faithful as your love is faithful; and may I abide in your love always. Amen.

13 MAY

Save us and help us

PSALM 60:1-5

[1] You have cast us off, O God, and broken us.
You have been angry; take us back.
[2] You shook the land and split it open;
bind up the rifts, for it trembles still.
[3] You have made your people drink a bitter draught;
you have given us wine that makes us drunk.
[4] You have raised a banner for those who fear you,
a rallying point beyond range of the bow,
[5] so that they may be saved;
save us and help us with your right hand.

At those times when I am bitterly disappointed, O Lord, I pray that you will be with me. When I am deep in selfish pursuits, draw me back into your selfless love. When I am broken, heal me; when I am lost, find me; when I am alone, comfort me. My enemies are strong,

Lord, but your right hand will defend me. In your never failing love I put my trust. Amen.

14 MAY

Through God we shall fight courageously

PSALM 60:6-12

[6] God has spoken from his sanctuary:
"I will share out Shechem in triumph,
and portion up the Vale of Succoth.
[7] Gilead is mine and Manasseh is mine;
Ephraim, my helmet; my sceptre, Judah;
[8] my washbowl, Moab;
I will make Edom mine;
I shout in triumph over Philistia."
[9] Who will lead me to the fortified city?
Who will guide me into Edom?
[10] Only you, who have rejected us.
You march no more, O God, with our ranks.
[11] Grant us help against the foe,
for human help is vain.
[12] Through God we shall fight courageously,
for he will trample down our foes.

The army of the faithful trusts in your strength, Lord. The whole universe is yours, so why do you delay in bringing all nations into your kingdom? Guide me in my daily battle against the forces of evil and walk with me on my road to your eternal city. If you are not with me, my battle is lost, but in you my defence is secure. Go before me, O God, in all my actions. Amen.

15 MAY

I long to stay in your tent forever

PSALM 61:1-5

[1] O God, hear my cry,
and listen to my prayer.
[2] From the ends of the earth
I call to you
with fainting heart.
Lead me to the rock
beyond my reach.
[3] For you are my refuge,
a strong tower against foes.
[4] I long to stay
in your tent forever
and find a refuge
beneath your wings.
[5] For you, O God,
have heard my vows;
you grant me the share
of those who fear your name.

Hear my prayer, O Lord, for my heart is failing. Safety seems to be beyond my grasp. My only refuge is in you, for you are my strength and hope. I long to remain with you forever: I long to shelter under your comforting wings. I have promised to serve you all my life, O God, but your grace is my only support. Grant me a place in your kingdom. Amen.

16 MAY

May the king sit before God forever

PSALM 61:6-8

[6] Prolong the days
of the king's life;
let his years continue
for age after age.
[7] May he sit enthroned
before God forever;
may your faithful and constant love
watch over him.
[8] Then I shall always
sing praise to your name,
and fulfil my vows
day after day.

You are the eternal King of heaven and earth, O God, and earthly kings are responsible to you. I pray that the rulers of this world may pursue your wisdom and your sacrificial love, so that the people in their care may know justice, peace and happiness. I praise your holy name with all my heart and soul. May all peoples give you praise. Amen.

17 MAY

My salvation comes from God

PSALM 62:1-8

[1] My soul finds rest in God alone;
my salvation comes from him.

[2] Only he is my rock, my safety,
my fortress where I may stand unshaken.
[3] How much longer will you mount the assault,
all gathered to throw your victim down,
this leaning wall, this toppling fence?
[4] They aim to topple him from his height.
They take delight in lies.
Their mouths are filled with blessings,
while cursing in their hearts.
[5] Find rest, my soul, in God alone;
all my hope comes from him.
[6] He alone is my fortress, my rock of safety;
I will not be shaken.
[7] My safety and honour depend on God;
my mighty rock, my refuge place.
[8] Trust him always, all you people;
pour out your hearts to him;
God is our refuge.

In you alone, O Lord, do I find respite from the assaults of the powers of evil. I abhor falsehood and hypocrisy, yet I am drawn into sin myself. But you are my rock and my fortress; and when you are with me I stand on firm ground. Nothing will shake my resolution if you abide with me, O God. May everyone learn to trust in your love. Amen.

18 MAY

You, O Lord, show faithful love

Psalm 62:9-12

[9] Ordinary people are empty air;
important people are a sham;

they come to nothing when weighed on scales;
when put together they are lighter than air.
[10] Do not trust in extortion,
or take pride in stolen goods;
however much your wealth may grow,
do not set your heart on it.
[11] One thing God has spoken,
two things I have heard:
that you, O God, are strong,
[12] that you, O Lord, show faithful love.
You reward all as their deeds deserve.

All the people in the world put together, O Lord, are but a breath of air compared with your eternal life. Yet you have chosen me, as you have chosen many others, because of your faithful love towards us. Therefore, I do not wish to be ashamed by falling into sin or by coveting wealth. All I desire, O God, is to know your love and to receive your merciful judgement when I have run my course. Amen.

19 MAY

Your faithful love is better than life

Psalm 63:1-5

[1] O God, you are my God, I search for you;
my eager heart thirsts for you;
my body longs for you
as in an arid, weary land.
[2] I have glimpsed you in the sanctuary,
and seen your power and glory.
[3] Your faithful love is better than life,

therefore my lips will praise you.
[4] I will bless you as long as I live,
and raise my hands in your name.
[5] My soul is sated as with rich food;
a song of praise is on my lips.

I have longed for your presence, O God, and I have thirsted for your living water. Sometimes I have caught a glimpse of your majesty and I have touched the hem of your glory. I praise you mightily because your word is life to me. I bless you with my whole heart because your name is so wonderful on my lips. When I sing your praises it is a delight and a joy to me. Amen.

20 MAY

I call you to mind in the hours of night

PSALM 63:6-11

[6] On my bed when I think of you
I call you to mind in the hours of night;
[7] for you have always been my help.
I sing for joy beneath your wings.
[8] I keep close to you,
your power upholds me.
[9] May those who plan to destroy my life
go down to the depths of the earth;
[10] may they be given to the sword
and end as jackals' food.
[11] But the king will rejoice in God;
all who swear by him will glory,
while liars' mouths will be stopped.

As I go to sleep each night, O Lord, I think of your wonderful love and I know the safety of being under the shelter of your wings. I pray that I may always feel close to you, that I may always be upheld by your strength. Help me when evil powers plot against me; and confirm me in my citizenship of your glorious kingdom. Hear my prayer, O Lord. Amen.

21 MAY

O God, protect my life

PSALM 64:1-4

[1] Hear me, O God, as I make my complaint,
    protect my life from the threat of my foe.
[2] Hide me from intrigues of the wicked,
    from the noisy mob of evil-doers.
[3] They sharpen their tongues like a sword
    and aim poisoned arrows of words.
[4] From cover they shoot down the innocent;
    they suddenly shoot, with nothing to fear.

The world is full of wickedness, O God, and no one is safe except through your caring providence. Protect me as I go through the actions of each day and watch over my dreams as I sleep each night. The arrows of Satan are sharp in my flesh and the tongues of his agents are poisonous in my ears. Keep me in innocence, O God, and turn aside the sword of evil. Amen.

22 MAY

Let the righteous rejoice in Yahweh

PSALM 64:5-10

[5] They support each other in evil plots
and plan how to hide their snares;
they say, "Who will see them?"
[6] They devise unjust deeds,
say, "Our schemes cannot fail!"
The human mind and heart is cunning.
[7] But God will shoot them with his arrows;
suddenly they will be wounded.
[8] He will turn their very own words against them
and bring them to ruin.
All who see them will shake heads in scorn.
[9] All people will fear,
and proclaim it God's work,
and meditate on what he has done.
[10] Let the righteous rejoice
and take refuge in Yahweh;
let all the honest of heart praise him.

Those who use guile to make wicked plans will be foiled, O God, by your unfailing judgement. The devious will be trapped by their own words, for you are against them. I seek simplicity of heart and reverence for your word. I love to contemplate the marvellous works of your creation. In you, O God, let righteous people rejoice, for you are the refuge of the honest heart. Amen.

23 MAY

Blessed are those whom you choose

Psalm 65:1-4

[1] Praise is your due, O God, in Zion;
all our vows will be paid to you.
[2] O you who hear prayer,
all people should come to you;
[3] when we are overwhelmed by sins,
only you can forgive them.
[4] Blessed are those whom you choose
and invite to live in your courts;
we are filled with the bounty of your house,
of your holy Temple.

I praise you with my whole heart, O Lord, and I ask for your grace to help me to keep my promise to serve you until the end of my life. I can do no good thing without your guidance and I pray that all people may hear your call to righteous living. I give you thanks for the privilege of belonging to your kingdom as I journey on my pilgrim way and also I thank you for all the good gifts you have given to me. Amen.

24 MAY

You answer us with awesome deeds

Psalm 65:5-8

[5] O God our Saviour, you answer us
with awesome deeds of righteousness;
you are the hope of the ends of the earth
and of the furthest seas.

[6] You formed the mountains by your power
and armed yourself with strength.
[7] You stilled the roaring of the seas,
the crashing waves and tumultuous nations.
[8] The furthest nations fear your signs;
your miracles inspire shouts of joy
where day dawns and night falls.

I praise you, O God, for your mighty deeds and for your continuing care of your wonderful creation. My hope for the future is in your hands, and I know that people of all nations place their trust in you. I pray for peace throughout the world and for a just sharing of all your bounteous gifts. I shout for joy at the miracle of each day, Lord, and I give you thanks and praise for the gift of life. Amen.

25 MAY

You crown the year with your bounty

PSALM 65:9-13

[9] You care for the earth and water it,
you fill it with riches;
the rivers of God are full of water
to make the land give the people grain.
[10] You soak its furrows and smooth its ridges,
soften it with rain and bless its crops.
[11] You crown the year with your bounty
and your harvest tracks trail plenty;
[12] the desert pastures are lush
and the hills are wreathed in joy;
[13] the meadows are covered with flocks

and the valleys are clothed with grain;
they shout and sing for joy.

How marvellous your creation is, O God! The richness and beauty of the earth are wonderful to my senses. The seasons are a joy, and the rhythms of seed time and harvest are deep within me. I pray that nations may share your bounty with other nations and I also pray that human beings may learn to care for this world and all it contains. Amen.

26 MAY

Come and see the wonders of God

PSALM 66:1-7

[1] Shout with joy to God, all earth,
[2] sing to the glory of his name,
glorify him with your praise,
[3] say to God, "How terrible are your deeds."
Your enemies cringe
before the might of your strength.
[4] All the earth bows down to you,
sings songs to you,
sings in praise of your name.
[5] Come and see the wonders of God,
his awesome deeds for the people of earth:
[6] he turned the sea into dry land,
and people crossed the river on foot,
where we rejoiced in him.
[7] He rules forever by his power;
his eyes keep watch on all the nations;
do not let rebels rise against him!

I thank you, O God, for the revelation of your holy word and for all the wonderful deeds you have performed through your chosen leaders and prophets. My heart is full of joy to know that your kingdom encompasses all nations and that all rulers are subject to you. Watch over the nations of the world, O Lord, and bring peace and prosperity for everyone to share. Amen.

27 MAY

For you, O God, have tested us

PSALM 66:8-15

[8] You nations, bless our God,
let the sound of his praise be heard;
[9] he preserves us among the living
and keeps our feet from slipping.
[10] For you, O God, have tested us,
refined us like silver;
[11] you let us be imprisoned,
and laid loads on our backs.
[12] You let foes ride us down,
we went through fire and water,
but you brought us through
to a place of plenty.
[13] I will come to your house with burnt offerings,
and fulfil my vows to you,
[14] vows my lips made and my mouth spoke
when I was in distress.
[15] I will sacrifice fat animals to you,
an offering of rams,
I will give bulls and goats.

For the times you have saved me from danger, O Lord, I give you thanks. For the hard lessons I have had to learn through my mistakes, I thank you. You have tested me and made me strong in the faith, and I pray for the grace to fulfil the promises I have made to you. May all peoples know your love and experience your saving power. O God, I praise you with soul and heart and mind. Amen.

28 MAY

Blessed be God

PSALM 66:16-20

[16] Come and hear, all you who fear God,
    and let me say what he did for me.
[17] I cried out aloud to him,
    his praise was on my tongue.
[18] If I had kept any guilt in my heart
    the Lord would not have listened.
[19] But truly God did listen
    and heard my voice in prayer.
[20] Blessed be God
    who has not withheld
    his faithful love from me.

I confessed my sin to you, O God, and you listened to my entreaty. I pray that everyone will hear the good news of your love. The praise in my heart is a witness to your watching care, and I shall praise you openly so that the whole world may know what you have done for me. You have taken away my guilt and healed me, Lord: may your name be blessed forever. Amen.

29 MAY

May all the nations praise you

PSALM 67:1-3

[1] May God be gracious to us and bless us,
and turn his face to shine upon us;
[2] that your ways may be known on earth,
and all nations may know your salvation.
[3] May the peoples praise you, O God,
may all the nations praise you.

I have known your gracious love, O God, and I bless your name for your providential care towards those who turn to you. May your light always shine upon me, though I am an unworthy servant. May all peoples come to know your saving grace, so that your praise may be sung constantly throughout the world. With all my heart I glorify your holy name. Amen.

30 MAY

The land has given its harvest

PSALM 67:4-7

[4] May the nations rejoice and sing for joy,
for you judge the peoples justly
and guide the nations of earth.
[5] O God, may the nations praise you,
may all the peoples praise you.
[6] The land has given its harvest,
God, our God has blessed us.
[7] God has blessed us,
that all the world may fear him.

For your justice and your love, O Lord, I praise you. It is wonderful that anyone who approaches you with reverence and sincere love will know your tender care. Guide all the rulers of the world, that your bountiful harvests may be justly shared, according to your will. Your blessing is like the sunshine upon the harvest field: your word is like a joyful spring. For all your good gifts, I thank you, O God. Amen.

31 MAY

Father of orphans, the widows' defender

PSALM 68:1-6

[1] May God arise and his foes be scattered,
may those who hate him flee before him.
[2] You blow them away like wind;
you melt them like wax near fire.
The wicked die near God.
[3] But the upright are joyful;
they exalt before God and cry out with joy.
[4] Sing to God, sing praise to his name,
extol him who rides on the clouds;
rejoice in Yahweh and dance before him.
[5] Father of orphans, the widows' defender,
such is God in his holy dwelling.
[6] God gives a home to the friendless,
he leads the prisoner to safety,
but rebels are left
in a sun-scorched land.

Scatter the dark clouds of sin and hate, O Lord, and shine your glorious light upon all the nations of the world. May the wicked stumble over their own wickedness and may they be changed by the challenge of your incredible love. May those in need experience your special grace, so that in the lonely imprisonment of their souls they may reach out to your glorious freedom. Amen.

1 JUNE

You marched at the head of your people

PSALM 68:7-19

[7] O God, when you marched at the head of your
people,
when you strode through the desert places,
[8] the earth shook and the heavens poured rain
at the presence of God,
the God of Israel.
[9] O God, you rained a shower of blessings;
your weary inheritance
was filled with strength.
[10] Your people settled, and in your goodness,
O God, you provided for the poor.
[11] Yahweh gave the command,
and great was the number
of those who proclaimed it:
[12] "Kings and their armies have fled in haste;
their camps are plundered
and the loot shared out.
[13] While you are asleep in the sheepfolds,
the wings of the dove are covered in silver,
her feathers with shining gold.
[14] When the Almighty routed the kings in the land
it was like snow falling on Zalmon."
[15] The hill of Bashan is a high hill;
an arrogant hill is the hill of Bashan!
[16] Why do you envy, you arrogant hills,
the mountain where God has chosen to live?
God will live there forever.
[17] The chariots of God are tens of thousands,
and thousands of thousands;

Yahweh has come to his Temple from Sinai.
[18] You have scaled the heights and taken captives;
all brought you tribute, even rebels,
that Yahweh God might have a dwelling.
[19] Blessed be Yahweh who carries us daily,
God our Saviour.

May you lead your faithful people through the deserts of our age, Lord, as you led the tribes of Israel through the wilderness in ancient times. May we, too, have a victory of the spirit, so that we may enter the promised land of your kingdom. Your angels are innumerable, O God, and I know they will defend those who love you. I thank you for helping me each day in my battle against the forces of evil. Amen.

2 JUNE

Our God is a God who saves us

PSALM 68:20-31

[20] Our God is a God who saves us;
from Yahweh God comes escape from death.
[21] God crushes the heads of his foes,
the matted head of the one who walks in wickedness.
[22] Yahweh has said, "I will fetch them from Bashan,
I will fetch them from the depths of the sea,
[23] that you may bathe your feet in blood
and your dogs lap your enemies blood."
[24] Your processions have come into view, O God;
parades of my God, of my King,
to the sanctuary.

[25] In front are the singers; behind them, musicians;
with them the maidens
playing on tambourines.
[26] Bless God in the great congregation;
let the assembly of Israel bless Yahweh.
[27] Led by the youngest, the tribe of Benjamin,
the princes of Judah wear bright-coloured robes,
the princes of Zebulun, the princes of Naphtali.
[28] Summon your might, O God;
show us your strength, O God,
as you did before.
[29] Kings will come to you bearing gifts
for the sake of your Temple
in Jerusalem.
[30] Rebuke the Beast of the Reeds,
that herd of bulls,
the bull-calf troops of the nations.
Make it bring bars of silver,
and prostrate itself.
Scatter the nations which revel in war.
[31] Envoys will come from Egypt;
Nubia will stretch out its hands to God.

I pray, O Lord, that all nations will come to know your word and that your victory over the powers of evil may be worldwide. I rejoice when I worship you in the company of the faithful, and I pray that soon all nations may bow down in prayer before your heavenly throne. The music of peace will echo throughout the world when you touch the hearts of all peoples. Hear my prayer, O God. Amen.

3 JUNE

You are awesome, O God

PSALM 68:32-35

[32] You kingdoms of earth, sing praises to God,
sing praise to the Lord,
[33] to him who rides the ancient skies,
who thunders with mighty voice.
[34] Proclaim the might of God,
Israel's pride,
the power enthroned in the skies.
[35] You are awesome, O God, in your sanctuary.
He is Israel's God.
He gives might and power
to his people.
Praise be to God.

May all the peoples of the earth worship you, O God. Your glory shines reflected on the clouds and your praise echoes way beyond the thunderclap of the last day. May all the faithful praise your awesome might: may all races worship in your holy sanctuary. I praise you with all my heart and soul, O Lord, for you are the King of heaven and earth. Amen.

4 JUNE

Save me, O God

PSALM 69:1-6

[1] Save me, O God,
for the waters are closing over me,

[2] I sink in the deepest swamp
where there is no firm ground;
I have come into deep waters,
and the flood overwhelms me.
[3] Exhausted with crying for help,
my throat is parched and my eyes fail,
searching for my God.
[4] Those who hate me for no reason
are more than the hairs of my head;
I have foes strong and treacherous,
who wish to destroy me.
Must I return what I did not steal?
[5] O God, you know how foolish I am,
for my guilt is not hidden from you.
[6] May none of those who hope in you
be shamed through me, O Lord Yahweh of Hosts;
those who seek you must not be disgraced,
because of me, O God of Israel.

Sometimes, O Lord, the cares of the world seem to take up all my energy and, when I seek you, I cannot find you. I fight against temptation and the powers of Satan and I seem to be surrounded by falsehood and treachery. You know all my sins and I can hide nothing from you, so I place my guilt in your hands, Lord, and pray for the grace of your vindication. Amen.

5 JUNE

I bear reproach for your sake

PSALM 69:7-15

[7] I bear reproach for your sake,
and shame has covered my face;
[8] I am cut off from my brothers,
a stranger to my mother's sons,
[9] for zeal of your house consumes me,
and insults to you fall on me.
[10] When I fast with bitter weeping,
it only leads to insults;
[11] when I go about in sackcloth,
people only laugh at me;
[12] I am mocked by idlers at the gate,
and I am the theme of drunken songs.
[13] But I pray to you, O Yahweh,
at an acceptable time;
in your great and faithful love,
O God, answer with sure deliverance.
[14] Rescue me from the swamp
and do not let me sink;
save me from those who hate me,
and from the deep waters.
[15] Do not let the floods engulf me
and the depths drown me,
and the pit close its mouth on me.

If quarrels with friends or my family overtake me, Lord, I pray that you will bring reconciliation. If those around me curse your name, help me to be strong in defence of my faith. If people laugh at my prayers, so fill me with your love that I may show love to my enemies. Save me from the swamps of despondency, O God, and be my sure refuge. Amen.

6 JUNE

O God, I am wounded and in distress

PSALM 69:16-29

[16] Answer me, O Yahweh,
for your faithful love is good;
turn towards me in tenderness.
[17] Do not turn your face from your servant,
answer me quickly, for I am in trouble;
[18] come near and save me,
set me free because of my foes.
[19] You know the insults, my shame and disgrace;
all who trouble me are well known to you.
[20] Scorn has broken my heart and left me despairing;
I vainly sought pity
and could not find comfort.
[21] They gave me poison to eat
and vinegar for my thirst.
[22] May their own table become a trap,
and their security a snare.
[23] May their eyes be darkened until they are blind
and their bodies be struck with trembling.
[24] Pour out your fury on them;
overtake them with burning anger.
[25] Turn their camp into ruins;
make their tents uninhabited;
[26] for they hound those you struck,
and hurt those you wounded.
[27] Charge them with crime upon crime,
and deny them a share of salvation.

[28] May they be scratched from the book of life,
and never be listed with the righteous.
[29] O God, I am wounded and in distress;
may your saving power protect me.

At times I am filled with hate of my enemies, O Lord, and I long for their destruction. I pray at such times that I may know your faithful love. Do not turn your face away from me and help me in my time of trouble. Give me the wisdom to allow you to judge and to deal with those who cause conflict. Grant me peace in my innermost sanctuary, O God. Amen.

7 JUNE

Yahweh hears the poor

PSALM 69:30-36

[30] I will praise God's name in song;
and glorify him with thanksgiving.
[31] This will please Yahweh more than a bull,
a young ox with horns and hooves.
[32] The humble will see and be glad;
take heart, all you who search for God;
[33] for Yahweh hears the poor,
and does not despise his exiled people.
[34] Let the heaven and earth give him praise,
the seas and everything in them,
[35] for God will rescue Zion,
and rebuild the cities of Judah.
People will settle and own their own land.
[36] His servants' descendants will inherit it,
and those who love his name
will live there.

The praise in my heart, Lord, is a continuing song of your glory. At the same time, I pray for genuine humility, that I may be worthy to approach the throne of your grace. I know that you care for the poor and neglected of your people and I ask for each of them also a rich blessing. May your kingdom come, O God, and may the whole earth praise your glorious name. I seek to dwell in your house forever. Amen.

8 JUNE

O Yahweh, come quickly

PSALM 70

[1] Be pleased, O God, to save me;
  O Yahweh, come quickly and help me.
[2] Put to shame and confusion
  all who seek my life;
repulse them in disgrace
  who try to do me hurt.
[3] Let those who shout "Aha!" at me
  be aghast with shame.
[4] But let all who seek you
  rejoice and be glad in you;
let them cry out eternally,
  they who love your salvation,
  "May God be exalted!"
[5] But I am poor and in need;
  come quickly to me, O God.
You are my helper, my saviour,
  O Yahweh, do not delay.

Be near me, O Lord, when I am put to shame by circumstances: help me when I am afraid and alone. Give me the strength to persevere in the face of all difficulties. May all who turn to you receive your grace and may all who sing your praise find their home with you. Only you, O God are my Saviour. When I am in despair lift up my heart by your presence. Amen.

9 JUNE

I have found refuge in you, O Yahweh

PSALM 71:1-14

[1] I have found refuge in you, O Yahweh,
let me never be put to shame.
[2] By the power of your righteousness
save and deliver me,
hear me and rescue me.
[3] Be a fortified rock for me,
where I can always go;
give the order to save me,
for you are my stronghold and rock.
[4] Deliver me, O God, from wicked hands,
from the grasp of the evil and cruel.
[5] For you are my hope, O Lord of all,
my trust, O Yahweh, since a child;
[6] from birth I relied on you;
you brought me from my mother's womb;
always, I sing your praise.
[7] I have become like a warning to many,
but I have you for my strong refuge.
[8] My mouth is full of your praise,
all day long declaring your splendour.

[9] Do not reject me in my old age;
do not desert me when strength has failed.
[10] For my foes speak against me;
conspirators plot my death,
[11] saying, "God has forsaken him;
chase him and seize him,
for no one will rescue him."
[12] O God, do not stand aloof;
O my God, come quickly and help.
[13] May my slanderers die in shame;
may those who wish me harm
be covered with scorn and disgrace.
[14] But as for me, I will always hope;
my praise for you will always grow.

You have watched my footsteps from childhood, O God, and without you I would have long ago come to grief deeper than I could bear. Stay with me throughout my life and guide me in all my thoughts and actions. When life seems perplexing or when the power of evil seems strong, come quickly to my help. My hope is entirely in you, O God. I praise you now and always. Amen.

10 JUNE

Who is like you, O God?

PSALM 71:15-21

[15] My mouth will speak of your righteousness,
and tell all day of your saving power,
it is past my skills to say it all.
[16] I will come and declare your mighty acts,

O Lord of all,
and proclaim your justice, yours alone.
[17] O God, you have taught me from my youth;
all my life I have told of your mighty acts.
[18] Even when I am old and grey,
do not desert me, O God,
until I have told of your strength
to generations still to come,
your might to all who are still to come.
[19] Your righteousness reaches the skies, O God,
you have done such great things, O God;
who is like you?
[20] You have shown me troubles,
many and bitter,
but you will restore my life again;
you will raise me again from the depths of earth.
[21] Restore me to honour;
give me comfort again.

Teach me from my experience, O Lord, and show me my errors, that I may learn your ways. I long to share the knowledge of your righteousness with others, and to tell of your saving power. May your justice prevail throughout the world and may future generations hear of the great things you have done for those who trust in you. You have restored me many times, O God, and I give thanks for the comfort of your love towards me. Amen.

11 JUNE

I will praise you for your constancy, O God

PSALM 71:22-24

[22] I will praise you on the harp,
  for your constancy, O God;
I will praise you with the lyre,
  O Holy One of Israel.
[23] My lips shout for joy as I sing to you,
  for you have redeemed me.
[24] All day long my tongue tells of your righteous
    deeds,
for those who would harm me
  are shamed and disgraced.

I praise you, O God, for your constant and wonderful love and for your repeated redemption of my sinful soul. I sing for joy at the thought of your righteous deeds. Before your holiness I bow my head in the deep consciousness of my unworthiness. Yet, O Lord, you allow me to come close to you in my prayers. Keep me from all harm and evil, this day, and always. Amen.

12 JUNE

That the king may rule your people with justice

PSALM 72:1-7

[1] O God, endow the king with your justice,
  the royal son with your righteousness,
[2] that he may rule your people with justice,
  and give fair judgement to your poor.

[3] The mountains will bring your people prosperity,
the hills will give them righteousness.
[4] He will be just with the poorest of people,
save the children of the poor
and crush the oppressor.
[5] You will be feared as long as the sun,
as long as the moon,
through all generations.
[6] He will come down like rain on a newly-mown field,
like showers that water the earth.
[7] In his days the righteous shall flourish,
and good fortune abound
until the moon is no more.

Grant, O Lord, that all earthly rulers may follow the pattern of your kingdom. May justice prevail and may all nations share in the riches of your creation. Protect the poor and needy and bring cruel rulers to the justice they deserve. May those who follow righteousness prosper and live forever in the kingdom of your love. Hear my prayer, O God, and fill my heart with your peace. Amen.

13 JUNE

He will pity the weak and the needy

PSALM 72:8-19

[8] He will rule from sea to sea,
from the river Euphrates
to the ends of the earth.
[9] The desert tribes will bow before him,
and his foes lick the dust.

[10] The kings of Tarshish and distant shores
will pay him tribute;
The kings of Sheba and Seba
will bring him gifts.
[11] All kings will bow before him,
and all nations serve him.
[12] He will free the needy who cry to him,
the afflicted who cannot get help.
[13] He will pity the weak and the needy,
and deliver the needy from death.
[14] From oppression and violence he will save them;
their blood will seem precious to him.
[15] May he live long and have gold from Sheba,
may prayer be made for him,
and blessings called down on him
all the day long.
[16] May wheat abound throughout the land,
swaying on hill-tops;
may fruit flourish like Lebanon,
and thrive like the grass of the field.
[17] May his name last for ever,
continue as long as the sun;
all nations will pray to be blessed as he is,
they will all say how blessed he is.
[18] Blessed be Yahweh God, the God of Israel,
who alone does marvellous things;
[19] may his glorious name be blessed for ever;
may all the earth be filled with his glory.

Your kingdom stretches from heaven to earth, O Lord, and encompasses the whole of your creation. May all earthly kings serve you and may the oppressed peoples be freed by your grace. Bring prosperity to the whole earth, O God, and may your name be praised forever. May all nations come to worship you and may all peoples come to know your glory. Amen.

14 JUNE

The wicked are carefree and piling up wealth

PSALM 73:1-12

[1] God indeed is good to Israel,
to those who are pure of heart.
[2] My feet had almost slipped,
I had nearly lost my foothold,
[3] for I envied the boasters
when I saw how the wicked prosper.
[4] They have no pain or suffering;
their limbs are sleek and strong;
[5] they are free from common troubles;
they do not suffer human ills.
[6] So pride is their necklace
and violence their clothing.
[7] Their callous hearts breed malice;
unending evil scheming fills their minds.
[8] Their talk is all mocking and malice;
they loftily threaten with force.
[9] Their mouths lay claim to heaven;
their tongues take possession of earth.
[10] So my people follow their lead
and lap up the waters of wealth.
[11] They say, "How can God ever know?
Does the Most High know or care?"
[12] That is what the wicked are like,
always carefree and piling up wealth.

Thank you, O Lord, for saving me from harm and danger. Yet, I ask for a deeper understanding of your ways, for it is hard to understand why the wicked often seem to prosper, while those who try to be good sometimes meet serious difficulties in their lives. Give me the wisdom, O God, follow a straight path in the midst of malice and hypocrisy, and strengthen me in my faith. Amen.

15 JUNE

I went into the house of God

Psalm 73:13-20

[13] Was it all for nought that I kept my heart pure;
did I wash my hands free from guilt in vain?
[14] All day long I was battered with blows,
and every dawn brought new punishment.
[15] But if I had said, "I shall talk like them",
I should have betrayed the children of God.
[16] When I set my mind to grasp all this
I found it all too hard for me,
[17] until I went into the house of God;
then I saw what their end would be.
[18] Indeed you place them on slippery ground,
and throw them headlong to their ruin.
[19] Suddenly they are destroyed
and swept away by total terror.
[20] As a dream dissolves when one awakes,
so, O Yahweh, when you arise,
you dismiss them as fantasies.

Confirm me in your ways, O God, and grant that I may endeavour by your grace to pursue a holy and pure life.

Only in your presence am I able to perceive the end of wickedness and deceit. Grant me a firm footing that I may not slide into the many temptations which assail me. Dismiss all evil dreams, O God, and grant me quietness of soul. Amen.

16 JUNE

You grasp my right hand

PSALM 73:21-28

[21] When my heart was grieved
and my spirit embittered,
[22] I was stupid and ignorant,
a mere beast before you.
[23] But even so, I stay in your presence,
you grasp my right hand,
[24] your counsel guides me,
and afterwards you will receive me with glory.
[25] Whom have I in heaven but you?
If I am with you,
I want nothing on earth.
[26] My flesh and my heart may fail,
but God is my heart's rock,
my portion forever.
[27] For those who abandon you will perish;
you destroy all who are unfaithful to you.
[28] But my chief good is to be near God;
I have made Lord Yahweh my refuge,
to tell of all your deeds.

Hold my hand, O Lord, and guide me from the ignorance of my former ways. You alone are my strength and salvation, and when you are with me I have no other need. When I am in danger of falling, you are my rock and you are my peace. Abide with me, O God, and be my refuge through all the vicissitudes of this life, that I may at the end of my days enter the courts of heaven. Amen.

17 JUNE

Remember the people you adopted

PSALM 74:1-11

[1] O God, why have you cast us off?
And will it be forever?
Why burn with anger
at the sheep of your pasture?
[2] Remember the people you adopted so long ago,
the tribe you redeemed to be your inheritance;
remember Mount Zion, the place where
you lived.
[3] Pick your way now through the unending ruins,
all the destruction foes brought on the
sanctuary.
[4] Your enemies roared in the place where you met
with us,
and set up their standards as tokens of victory.
[5] Like men wielding axes through thickets of trees,
[6] with axes and hatchets they smashed the carved
panelling;
[7] set fire to the sanctuary,
tore down and polluted the home of your
name.
[8] They said in their hearts, "We will crush them
completely!"

They burned every holy place all through
the land.
[9] We no longer see miracles, no prophets are left,
and none of us knows for how long this
will last.
[10] How long will you let the foe mock you, O God?
Will the enemy insult your name evermore?
[11] Why do you hold back your hand, your right
hand?
Take it out from the folds of your garment
and kill!

Sometimes, O Lord, it seems that your enemies are triumphant. They forsake the faith and they despise your sanctuaries. How long will it be before you challenge them? Where are the miracles to prove your presence and where are the prophets who will lead the nations to the truth? Only you, O God, have the power to change the world. I pray that your kingdom will come soon. Amen.

18 JUNE

O God, salvation throughout the earth

PSALM 74:12-17

[12] You, O God, are my king from the first;
source of salvation throughout the earth.
[13] It was you who divided the sea by your power;
you smashed the sea serpent's heads in the
waters;
[14] it was you who crushed the heads of Leviathan
and gave him as food to the beasts of the desert.

[15] You opened up channels for springs and torrents,
 and dried up streams that had flowed forever.
[16] Yours is the day and yours is the night,
 you established the sun and the moon.
[17] You alone fixed all the regions of earth;
 you created both summer and winter.

I thank you, O God, King of the universe, for all the wonders of creation. It is marvellous to me to think of the power of the oceans and the beauty of the changing seasons. You have placed the planets in their courses and yet they are merely fine dust among the galaxies you have made. You are my King and my Lord, and I worship you with my whole heart and mind. Amen.

19 JUNE

Show concern for your covenant

PSALM 74:18-23

[18] Remember, O Yahweh, the enemy's blasphemy,
 how foolish people poured scorn on your name.
[19] Do not abandon your dove to the wild beasts;
 forget not forever the sufferings of your people.
[20] Show concern for your covenant,
 because thoughts of violence
 fill all the dark places throughout the land.
[21] Do not let the oppressed have to flee in disgrace;
 may the poor and downtrodden
 give praise to your name.
[22] O God, rise up and defend your cause;
 remember fools mocking you all the day long.
[23] Do not ignore all the shouts of your enemies,
 the unending uproar made by your foes.

Your covenant is universal and everlasting, O Lord, and I rest on my faith in you, despite the mischief and wickedness of the world about me. I pray that the poor and oppressed may find succour in your wonderful and gracious love. The children of the faith are like doves before the ferocity of the ungodly, and I pray that you may protect all of them. Hear my prayer, O God. Amen.

20 JUNE

I am the one who judges justly

PSALM 75:1-5

[1] We thank you, O God, we give you thanks;
we call on your name
and recall your wonderful deeds.
[2] You say, "I choose the proper time,
I am the one who judges justly.
[3] When the earth quakes and all its people,
I am holding the pillars in place.
[4] I tell the proud to stop their boasting,
and the wicked to distrust their strength.
[5] Do not test your strength with the heavens;
do not talk with arrogant looks!"

I give thanks, O Lord, for all your good gifts and for all the wonderful things you have done for me. I await your judgement with the assurance of your love and forgiveness. I praise the majesty and power which holds together the structures of the universe. How could I ever boast in my own power, O God, when you are my Creator and Sustainer? I praise you with my whole heart. Amen.

21 JUNE

I will proclaim the God of Jacob forever

PSALM 75:6-10

[6] None from the east nor from the west;
none from the desert decides who has power.
[7] It is God who judges,
he brings one down
and exalts another.
[8] The hand of Yahweh bears a cup
filled with wine and spices;
he pours the wine, the wicked drink
and drain it to the dregs.
[9] But I will proclaim him forever;
I will sing in praise
to the God of Jacob.
[10] I will smash the power of the wicked,
but the power of the just
will be lifted high.

In all quarters of the earth, O Lord, no human being can have any power except by your will. Those who believe they have their own power owe it to you, and I pray that such rulers may learn responsibility in the light of your judgements. I know that those who act cruelly and with wicked intent will be brought down eventually by their own craftiness. I praise you for your judgements, O God, and I pray for a happy and peaceful world. Amen.

22 JUNE

You, O God, are radiant with light

PSALM 76:1-7

[1] God is known in Judah,
his name is great in Israel;
[2] his tent is in Salem,
his home is in Zion.
[3] There he broke the flashing arrows,
shields and swords,
and weapons of war.
[4] You are radiant with light,
more regal than the eternal hills.
[5] The brave lie plundered, in lasting sleep;
not one of the soldiers can lift his hands.
[6] O God of Jacob, at your rebuke,
both horse and chariot lie still.
[7] You alone strike terror.
Who can withstand you in your anger?

I pray, O Lord, that your name may be known throughout the world, so that all nations may praise you. Your kingdom is unassailable and the forces of Satan will never take your heavenly city. Your light is wonderful in my heart and the radiance of your presence accompanies my every day. No one can stand against you, O God, and your majesty and holiness are my daily praise. Amen.

23 JUNE

You O God, gave your judgement to save all

PSALM 76:8-12

[8] You pronounced your judgement from heaven;
the earth was afraid and was quiet,
[9] when you, O God, gave your judgement
to save all the poor of the land.
[10] Human wrath can only respect you;
you arm yourself with total wrath.
[11] Make vows to Yahweh your God and keep them,
let all the lands around
bring gifts to the One who is feared.
[12] He curbs the spirit of princes;
he fills the kings of the earth with fear.

Give me the grace, O God, to keep my promise to serve you throughout my life. Take away any unworthy self-pride from my heart. Protect the poor and curb the powerful that they may respect your holiness. Your judgements are certain, and unjust rulers will receive their deserts. Yet, I pray that all the leaders of the nations will bring their gifts to your altar. Hear my prayer, O Lord. Amen.

24 JUNE

Has the Lord's faithful love vanished forever?

PSALM 77:1-12

[1] I called to God for help
I called to God to hear me;

[2] when I was in trouble, I sought the Lord;
I stretched out untiring hands all night
but my soul could not be comforted.
[3] I think of you, O God, and groan;
I meditate, and my spirit faints.
[4] You keep my eyes from closing;
I am too distraught to speak.
[5] My thoughts return to times long past,
to years long gone;
[6] I recall my songs in the night,
and my spirit asks this question:
[7] "Will the Lord reject us forever,
and never show his favour again?
[8] Has his faithful love vanished forever,
and his promise ended eternally?
[9] Does God forget to show mercy;
has his anger shut off his compassion?
[10] This is what wounds me," I said,
"that the power of the Most High has
changed."
[11] I call to mind the wonders of Yahweh,
and remember your deeds in the past;
[12] I think about all that you did,
and consider all your great deeds.

I feel far away from you sometimes, Lord. I pray, but the inner light of my spirit is dim. Yet I know that you do not change, for your love is a steady flame that is never extinguished. I pray that you will open my eyes that I may see your presence in my daily life again. The wonders of this world you have created are many, and your mighty acts are marvellous to think about. How long, O Lord, how long? Hear my prayer, I beseech you. Amen.

25 JUNE

You are the God who works marvels

PSALM 77:13-20

[13] Your way, O God, is holy;
what God is as great as our God?
[14] You are the God who works marvels,
and makes nations acknowledge your power.
[15] You saved your people with a mighty arm,
the descendants of Jacob and Joseph.
[16] O God, the waters saw you,
the waters saw you and writhed,
the depths of the sea were troubled.
[17] The clouds burst with water;
the skies crashed with thunder;
your arrows flashed on every side.
[18] Your thunder was heard in the whirlwind,
your lightning lit up the world,
the earth trembled and quaked.
[19] Your road went through the sea,
your path through the great waters,
but your footprints could not be traced.
[20] You led your people like a flock
by the hand of Moses and Aaron.

Your holiness is beyond my understanding, O God, though I can see the wonderful things you have done. I thank you for your revelations recorded in the scriptures and for your mighty saving power. I pray that you will act again today to bring the nations into your kingdom. Redeem the world, O God, and redeem me also from my sins. May universal peace abound and may you lead your people into the promised land of heaven. Amen.

26 JUNE

Things we have heard and known

Psalm 78:1-8

[1] Hear my teaching, O my people;
pay attention to what I say.
[2] I will tell you a story with hidden meanings,
I will speak of the mysteries of the past,
[3] things we have heard and known
that our fathers told us.
[4] We will not hide them from their children,
but will tell the next generation
the glorious deeds of Yahweh,
his power, and the wonders he did.
[5] He created a witness in Jacob,
he established a law in Israel,
which he ordered our ancestors
to hand on to their descendants,
[6] for the next generation to know,
the children yet unborn,
for them to tell their children.
[7] Then they would trust in God
and would not forget his deeds
but always keep his commands.
[8] They would not be like their ancestors,
a stubborn, rebellious age,
whose hearts were disloyal to God,
with spirits unfaithful to him.

I long to learn more about the mysteries of your ways, O Lord. You have done marvellous things in past ages and you have done wonderful things for me. I ask your forgiveness for those times when I have not lived up to my calling and I renew my commitment to the faith this day. May I be a faithful witness to those around me so that others may be brought into your glorious kingdom. Amen.

27 JUNE

The people failed to keep God's covenant

PSALM 78:9-16

[9] The people of Ephraim, armed with bows,
turned tail on the day of battle;
[10] they failed to keep God's covenant
and would not live by his law;
[11] they forgot what he had done
and the marvels he had shown them.
[12] In their fathers' sight he did wonders
in the land of Egypt, the fields of Zoan.
[13] He parted the sea for them to pass through,
and heaped up water on either side.
[14] By day he led them with a cloud,
and by night with the light of fire.
[15] He split the desert rocks
to give water from limitless depths;
[16] he brought streams out of the rock,
and made water run like rivers.

Forgive me, O Lord, for my unfaithfulness and for my weakness in the face of temptation. I thank you for your guidance through the difficulties of my life and I pray for your continued guidance as I pursue my pilgrimage. Give me the water of life, O God, and help me through the desert ways of the spirit when I have lost my way. Hear my prayer. Amen.

28 JUNE

The people deliberately challenged God

Psalm 78:17-33

[17] But they went on sinning against him,
they defied the Most High in the desert.
[18] They deliberately challenged God
by demanding the food they wanted.
[19] They criticised God by saying,
"Can God spread a table in the desert?
[20] He made water gush when he struck the rock
and rivers flowed abundantly,
but can he also give us food?
Can he give his people meat?"
[21] When Yahweh heard them he was furious,
his fire blazed out against Jacob
and his anger rose against Israel,
[22] because they showed no faith in God,
and did not trust his saving power.
[23] But he still commanded the skies above
and opened the doors of heaven;
[24] he rained down manna for people to eat
and gave them the wheat of heaven;
[25] mortals ate the bread of angels;
he sent them all the food they could want.
[26] He loosed the east wind from heaven,
and sent the south wind by his power,
[27] to rain down meat like dust,
birds like the sand of the seas.
[28] He made them fall in the midst of their camp,
all around their tents,
[29] and they ate and were filled to the full,
for he gave them all they wanted.

[30] But before they had finishing eating,
while the food was still in their mouths,
[31] God's anger rose against them;
he killed the strongest of them,
and cut down the youth of Israel.
[32] Despite all this, they kept sinning;
despite his marvels, they did not believe,
[33] so he ended their days like mist
and their years in sudden terror.

May I trust in you always, O Lord, and in those times when my faith wavers I pray that you will abide with me. Grant me my daily needs and help me to see the difference between what is essential and what is unessential. May all the peoples of the world learn to share your good gifts and may all peoples learn to obey your commandment of love. Amen.

29 JUNE

The people's hearts were not loyal to him

Psalm 78:34-39

[34] Whenever God killed them they sought him,
and turned to him keenly again;
[35] they remembered that God was their rock,
God the Most High, their redeemer.
[36] They would flatter him with their mouths
but they lied to him with their words,
[37] for their hearts were not loyal to him
and they did not keep his covenant.
[38] And yet he showed them mercy,
he removed their iniquities,
and did not destroy them.

He often restrained his anger and kept back his
wrath.
[39] He knew they were only flesh,
a passing breeze that never returns.

I know that I pray most when I am in trouble, Lord, and I ask your forgiveness for that. Help me to seek a true spirituality which burns steadily in all circumstances. Forgive me for my shortcomings and grant me inward peace. My life is but a breath of wind, but yet I know you will always be with me, even when my years on earth are complete. Bless my remaining days, O God. Amen.

30 JUNE

The people forgot about his power

Psalm 78:40-55

[40] They often defied him in the desert
and grieved him in the wilderness!
[41] Again and again they challenged him,
provoking the Holy One of Israel.
[42] They forgot about his power,
and the day he ransomed them from the foe,
[43] the time he showed his signs in Egypt,
his marvels in Zoan's fields.
[44] He turned their rivers to blood,
so they could not drink from their streams.
[45] He sent them swarms of biting flies
and frogs to cause them devastation.
[46] He gave their crops to caterpillars,
and the fruit of their work to locusts.

[47] He killed their vines with hail,
their sycamores with frost.
[48] He abandoned their cattle to hail,
and their flocks to thunderbolts.
[49] He unleashed his fury on them,
wrath, indignation and trouble,
a troop of destroying angels.
[50] He made a road for his anger
and did not spare them from death
but delivered them to the plague.
[51] He struck down all first-born in Egypt,
the first of their strength in the country of Ham.
[52] But he brought out his people like sheep,
and led them like a flock through the desert.
[53] He led them in safety without any fear,
but the sea engulfed their foes.
[54] He brought them to his holy land,
the hills his own right hand had won.
[55] He drove out nations before them
and gave them their lands as a heritage,
he put Israel's tribes in their tents.

For the times when you have saved me from danger, I thank you, O Lord. For the times when you have forgiven my complaining and my selfishness, I give you thanks. Guide me each day and deliver me from the servitude of sin and from the power of evil. Bring me into your kingdom, O God, and walk before me as I journey. Keep me in safety, this day and always. Amen.

1 JULY

The people still challenged God

PSALM 78:56-64

[56] But they still challenged God,
rebelled against the Most High
and did not keep his statutes.
[57] They were treacherous and faithless like their
ancestors,
as unreliable as a twisted bow.
[58] Their high places made him angry;
they made him jealous with their gods.
[59] When God heard them he was furious
and rejected Israel completely.
[60] He left his dwelling at Shiloh,
the tent where he lived among mortals
[61] and abandoned his power to captivity,
his glory to enemies' hands.
[62] He delivered his people to the sword,
and loosed his anger on his heritage.
[63] Young men were eaten by fire;
their maidens had no wedding songs;
[64] their priests were put to the sword,
and their widows did not mourn.

Render me not what I deserve, O God, for all my misdoings, but grant me your abundant grace that I may dwell in your kingdom forever. Deliver me not into the hands of my enemies, but protect me from all harm and evil. Bless the community in which I live and create a loving spirit among your people. I desire to praise you and worship you always. Amen.

2 JULY

Then Yahweh chose David his servant

Psalm 78:65-72

[65] Then Yahweh rose as if from sleep,
like a strong man waking after wine,
[66] and routed all his enemies;
he put them to eternal shame.
[67] Rejecting the tents of Joseph,
ignoring the tribe of Ephraim,
[68] he chose the tribe of Judah,
his beloved hill of Zion.
[69] He built his sanctuary like the high mountains,
like the earth he had set firm forever.
[70] He chose David his servant,
and took him from the sheepfolds;
[71] he took him from tending sheep
to be shepherd of Jacob his people,
of Israel, his inheritance.
[72] With upright heart he tended them,
and guided them with skilful hands.

As you chose King David to be the shepherd of your people, O God, and gave him the wisdom to rule, so abide with me and give me the grace to fulfil my calling. Arise and scatter the darkness that besets me and let your light shine upon me all my length of days. Give me an upright heart and a spirit of love, that I may be worthy to enter your eternal kingdom. Amen.

3 JULY

O God, the nations have invaded your heritage

PSALM 79:1-4

[1] O God, the nations have invaded your heritage,
defiled your Temple
laid waste to Jerusalem.
[2] They have given your servants' corpses
for food to the birds of the air,
the bodies of your faithful
are given to the wild beasts.
[3] They have spilt blood like water
all around Jerusalem;
none is left to bury the dead.
[4] We are our neighbours' scorn,
mocked and derided
by those around us.

Be with me in times of tragedy, Lord. When the world is full of violence and war, grant your faithful followers succour. So many people seem to hate your name, and yet I am certain you are with those whom you have called. Why do you allow so much evil and wickedness in the world, O God? Bring peace in this age and protect those who praise your holy name. Amen.

4 JULY

Come quickly to meet us

PSALM 79:5-8

[5] O Yahweh, how long will your anger last?
Forever?

How long will your jealousy
burn like fire?
[6] Pour down wrath on nations
which do not know you,
on the kingdoms
which do not worship you,
[7] for they have devoured Jacob
and destroyed his home.
[8] Do not count our ancestors' sins
against us;
let your mercy
come quickly to meet us,
for we are in desperate need.

May all nations come to worship you, O God, and may your just wrath not consume the disobedient and wicked. Your mercy and forgiveness are needful when so many have sinned against your name. For my part, my past sins are ever before me, and I can only commend myself and others into your loving care. Have mercy, O God, have mercy. Amen.

5 JULY

Let the prisoners' groans rise before you

PSALM 79:9-13

[9] O God our Saviour, help us
for the glory of your name;
deliver us; forgive our sins,
for the sake of your name.
[10] Why should the nations ask,
"Where is their God?"

Let us see your servants' blood
avenged among the nations.
[11] Let the prisoners' groans rise before you;
by your arm's strength,
save the condemned.
[12] O Yahweh, heap on our neighbours
seven times their insults to you.
[13] Then we your people,
the sheep of your pasture,
will praise you forever;
from age to age
we will tell your praise.

Deliver me from my sins, O Lord: redeem me from my many transgressions. Have pity on those who are imprisoned and yet have done no wrong; and also on those who are enchained by their own selfishness. Why do you allow so many people to insult your sacred name, O God? Arise and protect your people and they will glorify you forever. Amen.

6 JULY

O God, bring us back

PSALM 80:1-7

[1] Hear us, O Shepherd of Israel,
leading Joseph like a flock;
shine forth enthroned,
sitting between the cherubim.
[2] Stir up your might
at the head of Ephraim,
Benjamin and Manasseh,
and come to save us.

[3] O God, bring us back;
make your face shine upon us
that we may be saved.
[4] O Yahweh, God of Hosts,
how long will you be angry
at your people's prayers?
[5] You have fed them
the bread of tears;
you have made them
drink many tears.
[6] You have made us
the scorn of our neighbours,
a laughing-stock to our enemies.
[7] O God of Hosts, restore us;
make your face shine upon us
that we may be saved.

I am sometimes mournful, Lord, because I seem to be far from your kingdom. May your face shine upon me at such times, that I may be saved from despair. You are my Shepherd and my King, O God, and in you I put my trust. Restore me and fill me with the Spirit of your love. May your angels watch over me by day and by night, now and forever. Amen.

7 JULY

You brought a vine out of Egypt

PSALM 80:8-13

[8] You brought a vine out of Egypt.
You drove out the nations
and planted it.

[9] You cleared the ground for it;
it took root
and filled the land.
[10] It covered the mountains with shadow;
its branches covered
the mighty cedars.
[11] It sent out branches
to the Sea,
its shoots as far as the River.
[12] Why have you smashed its walls
so that all who pass by
pick its grapes?
[13] Forest boars tear at it;
wild animals feed on it.

I thank you, O Lord, for tending your faithful people as a gardener tends a vine. Bless the many branches of your kingdom upon earth and guard your vineyard from the savage assaults of Satan. May your kingdom be universal so that all nations may be part of the true vine. Hear my prayer, O God, and bring peace and love to all peoples. Amen.

8 JULY

Grant us life

PSALM 80:14-19

[14] O God of Hosts, return to us;
look down from heaven and observe;
visit this vine,
[15] the root your right hand planted,
the son you reared for yourself.

[16] Your vine is cut down
and burned with fire;
your people perish
at your rebuke.
[17] Grant your power
to the one you trust,
the son of man
whom you reared for yourself.
[18] Then we will never turn back from you;
grant us life,
and we will call on your name.
[19] O Yahweh God Almighty, restore us;
let your face shine upon us
that we may be saved.

Return to me, O Lord, and make me fruitful on the vine of your great and wonderful love. I am lost if you forsake me: I am as nothing if you are not with me. Grant me the power each day to be your child, whom you created in the womb. Renew me in my love for you and grant me the blessing of life in your kingdom. Hear my prayer, O God. Amen.

9 JULY

Sing for joy to God our strength

PSALM 81:1-7

[1] Sing for joy to God our strength;
acclaim the God of Jacob.
[2] Start a melody, beat the drum,
play the tuneful lyre and harp.
[3] Blow the new moon in with rams' horns,

the full moon of our pilgrim-feast!
[4] This is a law of Israel,
a statute from the God of Jacob.
[5] He made it a law for Joseph
at the Exodus from Egypt,
where we heard a tongue we did not know.
[6] He says, "I lifted the load from his shoulders,
his hands were freed from the builder's load.
[7] You called in distress, so I rescued you,
and answered from the thundercloud;
I tested you at the waters of Meribah."

My heart is full of joy, O Lord, and I sing your praises with my whole heart. I love to worship you in the community because your faithful people can express their wonder together. It is marvellous, indeed, that you respond to all who turn to you. For your past acts of mercy I give thanks and for giving me strength in testing times I am full of gratitude. I praise you, O God. Amen.

10 JULY

If my people would only listen to me

PSALM 81:8-16

[8] "Listen, my people, to the warning I give you:
if you would only hear me, O Israel!
[9] You must not have any strange gods among you;
you must not worship an alien god.
[10] I am Yahweh your God,
who brought you out from Egypt.

You have only to open your mouth
and I fill it.
[11] But my people would not listen to me;
Israel would have none of me.
[12] So I gave them over to their stubborn hearts,
to follow their own devising.
[13] If my people would only listen to me,
if Israel would only follow my ways,
[14] how quickly would I subdue their enemies
and turn my hand against their foes.
[15] Those who hate Yahweh would plead for mercy,
although their doom was sealed forever.
[16] But you would be fed with the finest wheat,
and be filled with honey from the rock."

Forgive me, O God, when I have a stubborn heart. If ever I am tempted to centre my life on false values, guide me back to the straight path. I give you thanks for the daily bread which so often I take for granted and I pray that all peoples may have a fair share of your bounty. Grant me victory over the powers of evil, O God, and watch over my path. Amen.

11 JULY

How much longer will you judge unjustly?

Psalm 82

[1] God presides in the great assembly;
in the midst of the gods
he pronounces judgement:
[2] "How much longer
will you judge unjustly, and favour the wicked?

[3] Give the weak and the orphan justice,
be fair to the poor and oppressed.
[4] Save the weak and needy,
from the hand of the wicked."
[5] They know nothing and understand nothing;
they walk in darkness
while the earth's foundations rock.
[6] I thought you were gods,
all of you sons of the Most High.
[7] But you will die like mortals,
you will fall like every ruler.
[8] O God, rise up
and judge the world,
for all the nations
are your heritage.

There is no truth but you, O Lord: there is no power in heaven or earth except by your grace. Grant to those in need the justice they deserve and protect them from the powerful and wicked, from those who think they will rule forever. May your judgement against the unrighteous come soon, O God; and may all nations repent and turn to you in love. Amen.

12 JULY

Your foes plot against you

Psalm 83:1-12

[1] O God, do not keep silent,
not quiet, O God, not still.
[2] See how your enemies
raise an uproar,

how your foes
rear up their heads.
[3] They are making plans
against your people,
plotting together
against those you love.
[4] "Let us finish them
as a nation," they say,
"that Israel's name
may be known no more."
[5] With one mind
they plot together,
to form a league
against you,
[6] the tents of Edom, Ishmael and Moab,
and Hagar's kin,
[7] Gebal, Ammon and Amalek,
Philistia and the people of Tyre.
[8] Assyria too has joined them,
to strengthen the offspring of Lot.
[9] Treat them as you did Midian,
as Sisera and Jabin
at Kidron's river,
[10] who perished at Endor
to be dung on the ground.
[11] Make their leaders
like Oreb and Zeeb,
all their princes
like Zebah and Zalmunna,
[12] who said, "Let us take for ourselves
God's pasture."

Many plot against your servants, Lord, for the hearts of your enemies are hard and unloving. I pray that the overambitious may be curbed in their quest for power and that their plans to defeat the faithful may be foiled. Grant me the strength to fight for good and to cleanse myself from sin; to act with love and to hate evil; to search for your peace and to control my selfish passions. Hear my prayer, O God. Amen.

13 JULY

O Yahweh, cover their faces with shame

PSALM 83:13-18

[13] Make them like whirling dust,
O my God,
like chaff caught in the wind.
[14] As a forest fire
or a mountain blaze,
[15] drive them away
with your storm;
terrorise them
with your whirlwind.
[16] Cover their faces with shame,
until, O Yahweh,
they seek your name.
[17] May they always know
shame and terror;
may they perish in disgrace.
[18] Let them know it is you,
whose name is Yahweh,
who alone is Most High
over all the earth.

You alone, O God, command the powers behind the universe: you alone rule over the stars in their courses. I praise you for your glory. Yet, you allow evil powers to hold sway in earthly empires. I pray that the rule of the wicked may end, that their power may be whirled away like chaff in the wind. May they show repentance for their evil deeds; may they turn to you in reverence and may they learn the ways of loving worship. Amen.

14 JULY

Blessed are they who live in your house

PSALM 84:1-4

[1] How lovely is your dwelling-place,
O Yahweh of Hosts!
[2] With all my being I yearn and long
for the courts of Yahweh.
My whole being sings for joy
to the living God.
[3] Even the sparrow has found a home,
and the swallow has made a nest
for her young,
near your altar, O Yahweh of Hosts,
my King and my God.
[4] Blessed are they who live in your house,
they are always praising you.

I love to enter your sanctuary, O Lord, and I long to spend my time with you. Yet, the whole universe is your dwelling place and my body is your temple. I worship you with my whole heart and soul, and my mind is full of your praise every day. It will be wonderful, by your grace, to come to the courts of heaven and to worship you with all saints and all angels. May your kingdom live in me always. Amen.

15 JULY

Blessed are they who trust in you

PSALM 84:5-12

[5] Blessed are they
who have you for their strength,
whose hearts are set on pilgrimage.
[6] As they go through the Valley of Balsam
Yahweh makes it a place of springs;
the early rains fill it with pools.
[7] They go from strength to strength
and God shows himself to them in Zion.
[8] O Yahweh, God of Hosts, hear my prayer;
O God of Jacob, listen to me.
[9] Behold our shield, O God,
show favour to your anointed one.
[10] One day in your courts
is better than a thousand spent elsewhere;
I would rather live in the porch of God's house
than live in the tents of the wicked;
[11] for Yahweh God is a sun and a shield;
Yahweh bestows grace and glory.
He refuses nothing good
to those who live a blameless life.
[12] O Yahweh Almighty,
blessed are they who trust in you.

Strengthen me on my pilgrimage through life, O God, and guide my footsteps to the gates of heaven. Be my shield through all the chances and changes of each day. Grant that I may have the vision of your glory constantly before my eyes. Guard my paths so that I do not enter into wicked ways and strengthen my resolve when temptation assails me. Grant me your blessing, O Lord, that I may lead a blameless life. Amen.

16 JULY

Bring us back, O God our Saviour

PSALM 85:1-7

[1] O Yahweh, you showed favour to your land;
you brought back the captives of Jacob.
[2] You took away the guilt of your people
and covered all their sins.
[3] You retracted all your fury
and turned from your hot anger.
[4] Bring us back, O God our Saviour,
and cancel your displeasure.
[5] Will you be angry with us for ever?
Will your fury stretch on for age after age?
[6] Will you not give us life again,
that your people may rejoice in you?
[7] O Yahweh, show us your faithful love
and grant us your salvation.

Often you have rescued me from my sins, O Lord, and you have brought me back into your kingdom. Yet, I fall again and I have to turn to you for forgiveness. Renew me in your grace and cleanse me from my iniquities. My life is completely in your care and I pray that you will breathe into my soul the whisper of your love. Save me, O God, when I have lost my way. Amen.

17 JULY

Yahweh promises peace to his people

PSALM 85:8-13

[8] Let me hear the words of Yahweh God:
he promises peace to his people, his faithful,
if only they renounce their folly.
[9] His sure salvation is near those in awe of him,
so that his glory may dwell in our land.
[10] Love and faithfulness meet together;
peace and righteousness have embraced.
[11] Faithfulness rises up from the earth,
and righteousness looks down from heaven.
[12] Yahweh himself will give what is good,
and our soil will yield its harvest.
[13] Righteousness prepares his way,
treading out a path.

Speak to me, O Lord, in the depths of my soul, that I may know the fullness of your glory. Grant me that inward peace which is so wonderful to experience when you are near me. May the light of your love and the crown of your righteousness go with me, wherever I may journey, in this life or the next. May my life bear fruit in heaven when your call comes to me. Hear my prayer, O God. Amen.

18 JULY

You are full of faithful love

PSALM 86:1-7

[1] Listen to me, O Yahweh, and answer me,
for I am poor and in need.
[2] Guard me, for I am faithful to you;
save your servant who trusts in you,
for you are my God.
[3] O Yahweh, take pity on me,
for I call all day long to you.
[4] Bring joy to your servant,
for I lift up my heart to you.
[5] You are kind and forgiving, O Yahweh,
full of faithful love
to all who call to you.
[6] O Yahweh, hear my prayer,
and listen to my cry for mercy.
[7] In my day of distress I call to you,
and you will answer me.

I am poor in spirit, O Lord, and I need your guidance and help. Watch over me, for I have put my trust in you. When you come to me, my heart sings for joy, because your glory fills my whole being. Your grace and forgiveness are wonderful in my experience, and I pray to you with confidence and certainty. Visit me again, O God. Hear my prayer. Amen.

19 JULY

Grant me an undivided heart

PSALM 86:8-17

[8] Of all the gods, O Yahweh,
not one is like you;
no deeds can compare with yours.
[9] All nations will come and adore you, O Yahweh,
and give the glory to your name;
[10] for you are great and do wonderful deeds,
you alone, O God, and no other.
[11] Teach me your ways, O Yahweh,
that I may walk in your truth;
grant me an undivided heart,
that I may fear your name.
[12] With all my heart I will sing your praise,
O Yahweh my God;
I will glorify your name forever;
[13] for great is your faithful love for me,
you have saved my soul
from the depths of the grave.
[14] The proud are attacking me, O God;
my life is sought by a ruthless gang
which gives no thought to you.
[15] But you, O Lord God, are compassionate and faithful,
slow to anger,
rich in faithful love and constancy.
[16] Turn, then, and pity me;
grant your servant your strength
and rescue your maidservant's son.
[17] Give me a sign of your favour
that my foes may see

and be put to shame;
for you, O Yahweh, help me and comfort me.

No powers in heaven or on earth can be compared to you, O God. You are the One Lord, the only true God. Your works are wonderful and your glory is everlasting. I long to learn your ways and to walk in your light. May my heart be whole in your service and may I not be distracted by the power of sin. Your compassion and faithfulness are unending and I am hopeful of your help in my time of need. Help me and comfort me, O Lord. Amen.

20 JULY

All my inspiration is found in you, city of God

PSALM 87

[1] The city Yahweh founded
stands on the holy hill;
[2] Yahweh loves the gates of Zion
more than all the houses of Jacob.
[3] Glorious things are said about you,
city of God.
[4] I count Rahab and Babylon
among those who acknowledge me.
They say of Philistia, Tyre and Cush,
"This one was born there."
[5] But of Zion it will be said,
"All these were born in her,
and the Most High himself
will keep her secure."
[6] Yahweh himself will write the record

in the Book of the Nations,
"This one was born in Zion!"
[7] Singers and dancers alike will acclaim,
"All my inspiration is found in you."

The foundations of your kingdom are firm, O Lord: your holy city is glorious to behold. Your kingdom is both within me and before me, and I pray that I may learn the citizenship of heaven. May all nations and peoples come into your city and may the whole world praise your holy name. Inspire me with a vision of the heavenly Jerusalem, O God. Amen.

21 JULY

May my prayer reach your presence

PSALM 88:1-12

[1] O Yahweh, God of my salvation,
day and night I cry before you;
[2] May my prayer reach your presence,
turn your ear to my cry.
[3] For my soul is full of trouble,
my life is on the edge of the grave;
[4] I am counted with those who go down to the pit.
I am like a man who has lost his strength,
[5] left alone with the dead,
like the slaughtered in the grave,
the ones you no longer hold in mind,
cut off from your protection.
[6] You have placed me in the lowest pit,
in the darkest parts of the depths.
[7] I am weighed down by your heavy wrath;

you have overwhelmed me with all your waves.
[8] You have taken me from my closest friends
and made me utterly loathsome to them.
I am trapped and cannot escape;
[9] my eyes are dim with grief.
O Yahweh, I call to you every day,
and stretch out my hands to you.
[10] Do you work wonders for the dead?
Do the dead rise up in your praise?
[11] Is your love proclaimed in the grave,
your faithful love in destruction?
[12] Are your wonders known in the realms of darkness,
or your righteous acts in the land of oblivion?

I am blind and deaf to your presence, Lord, and I pray in vain for a sign. Yet, I know that you are never far away. In those times when I seem to be alone and lost, I pray that you will find me, for I cannot search you out. When I am miserable, give me the grace to count the many blessings you have given me. When I am in the dark, let the light of your love shine upon me. Amen.

22 JULY

I cry to you for help, O Yahweh

PSALM 88:13-18

[13] But I cry to you for help, O Yahweh;
my prayer comes before you every dawn.
[14] Why, O Yahweh, do you rebuff me,
why do you hide your face from me?
[15] Afflicted and close to death since childhood,
I have borne your terrors but now I despair.

[16] Your wrath has swept over me,
your terrors destroyed me;
[17] all day long they surge around me,
from every side they have flooded over me.
[18] You have taken from me my friends and
companions;
now darkness is my closest friend.

Each morning I turn to you, O Lord, and each day I desire to journey with you. Yet sometimes you seem to be far from me and I am afraid. Time takes away many friends and the thought of death is close. My only hope is in you, O God. Pierce this darkness with your glorious light and lift me into the realm of heaven. May I know your love always. Amen.

23 JULY

I will make known your constancy

Psalm 89:1-14

[1] I will sing Yahweh's faithful love forever;
I will make known your constancy
from age to age.
[2] I will declare that your love lasts forever,
you have fixed your constancy firm in heaven.
[3] "I have made a covenant
with the one I have chosen;
I have sworn an oath to my servant David:
[4] I will establish your line forever,
make your throne secure through all
generations."
[5] Your wonders are praised by the heavens, O Yahweh;

the gathering of the faithful
exalts your constancy.
[6] Who in the skies can compare with Yahweh?
Who like Yahweh in the court of heaven?
[7] The council of holy ones has great awe of God,
he is more feared than all who surround him.
[8] Who can compare with you, O Yahweh God
Almighty?
You are mighty, O Yahweh,
your constancy surrounds you.
[9] You rule the raging of the sea;
you curb its mounting waves.
[10] You crushed and killed the Rahab monster
and scattered your foes with your right arm.
[11] The heavens are yours and the earth is yours;
you made the world and everything in it.
[12] You created the north and the south;
Tabor and Hermon rejoice at your name.
[13] Strong of arm and strong of hand,
with right hand raised,
[14] your throne is built
on righteousness and justice;
faithful love and constancy
prepare your way.

I praise your eternal and faithful love, O Lord, and I give thanks for the covenant you have made with your people. With the whole company of heaven I worship you, for you have created all that is or ever will be. Your ways are wonderful to me, O God, for your holiness and righteousness go hand in hand with your love and your forgiveness. I will rejoice in your glory forever. Amen.

24 JULY

Blessed those who walk in your light, O Yahweh

PSALM 89:15-18

[15] Blessed are those who have learned to acclaim you,
 who walk in the light of your face, O Yahweh.
[16] They rejoice in your name all the day long,
 and are raised up by your righteousness;
[17] for you are their glory and strength,
 and by your favour we hold our heads high.
[18] To Yahweh belongs our shield,
 our king to Israel's Holy One.

May I walk in your light forever, O God, and may your face shine upon me. I rejoice in your name and I glorify you for your righteousness. Be my strength this day and grant me your abundant grace in all that I think or speak or do. You are my shield, O Lord, and I thank you for your gracious protection. O holy One, abide with me. Amen.

25 JULY

You are my rock

PSALM 89:19-29

[19] You spoke once in a vision,
 and said to your faithful people,
"I have given a warrior strength;
I have raised up a youth
 from the midst of the people.
[20] I have found David, my servant,

and anointed him with my sacred oil.
[21] My hand will support him,
and my arm will strengthen him.
[22] No enemy will be able to humble him,
no wicked man will bring him low.
[23] I will crush his foes before him,
and strike down those who hate him.
[24] My faithful love and constancy
will be with him,
by my name he will hold his head high.
[25] I will grant him power over the sea,
his right hand over the rivers.
[26] He will say to me, 'You are my father,
my God, my rock where I am saved.'
[27] So I will make him my first-born,
the highest of all earth's kings.
[28] My faithful love remains with him forever,
and my covenant with him will never fail.
[29] I will establish his line forever,
his throne will last as long as the heavens."

As you were with King David and his people, O Lord, so be with your faithful people today. You have anointed me with gladness because I know you are with me. Strengthen me to face the problems and perils of my daily life. May your faithful love and constancy be with me always. You are the Rock and the Father of those who have accepted your covenant. Be with me this day and forever. Amen.

26 JULY

I will not go back on my covenant

PSALM 89:30-37

[30] "If his children depart from my law
and do not obey my statutes,
[31] if they disobey my decrees
and fail to keep my commands,
[32] I will punish their sin with the rod,
their guilt with the whip;
[33] but I will not withdraw my faithful love from him,
nor swerve from my constancy.
[34] I will not go back on my covenant;
I will not withdraw my spoken word.
[35] Once and for all, I have sworn by my holiness,
I will keep faith with David.
[36] His line will continue before me forever,
his throne will last as long as the sun;
[37] it will stand firm forever, like the moon,
the faithful witness in the sky."

Help me to keep your law of love, O God, and guide me in my actions each day. When I fail to keep your commandments, grant me forgiveness and inner peace. I am aware of your faithful love surrounding the whole world and so, with all the saints and angels, I praise you and thank you that you care for me and that you help me to grow. May I be a faithful witness to your love, O God. Amen.

27 JULY

You have spurned your anointed one

Psalm 89:38-45

[38] Yet you have spurned your anointed one,
rejected him and raged at him,
[39] renounced the covenant with your servant,
and defiled his crown in the dust.
[40] You have breached all his walls,
and laid his strongholds in ruins;
[41] every by-passer plunders him,
his neighbours treat him with scorn.
[42] You have raised high his foes' right hand,
made all his enemies rejoice;
[43] You have turned back the edge of his sword
and deserted him in battle.
[44] You have stripped him of his splendour
and cast his throne to the ground.
[45] You have aged him before his time
and clothed him with shame.

Grant me the grace to accept less happy times with equanimity, O Lord, and give the humility to withstand the insults and scorn which sometimes come to your servants. Fill me with your love and peace so that, whatever life brings to me, I may stand and not fall. While I have my physical powers, may I use my energy positively; but when I am old and frail, help me to be strong within. Hear my prayer, O God. Amen.

28 JULY

Remember, O Lord, how brief is my life

PSALM 89:46-52

[46] How long will you hide yourself, O Yahweh?
Forever?
How long will your wrath flare up?
[47] Remember how brief is my life.
For what pointless end
did you make all people?
[48] Who can live without facing mortality?
Who can defy the power of the grave?
[49] Where are those former acts of faithful love,
you swore by your constancy to David,
O Yahweh?
[50] Remember, O Lord, how your servant is mocked,
how I bear in my heart the taunts of all nations,
[51] the taunts, O Yahweh, of your foes' mockery.
Your anointed is taunted at every step.
[52] Blessed be Yahweh forever.
Amen and Amen.

Reveal yourself to me, O Lord, that I may know you are with me. My life is dead without you. Unless I meet you each morning I am leading a pointless existence. Many of those around me do not seek you, but they seem not to care. Yet, I know that you love all your creation. I pray for my neighbours and for myself that you will bless all of us. I am assured that your love never fails, O God. Amen.

29 JULY

You are God from eternity to eternity

PSALM 90:1-9

[1] O Lord, you have been our dwelling-place,
throughout the ages.
[2] Before the mountains were made,
before you formed the earth and the world,
you are God from eternity to eternity.
[3] You turn people back to dust,
saying, "Go back to dust,
you children of mortals",
[4] for in your sight a thousand years
are like a passing day,
are like an hour of night.
[5] You brush mortals away like a dream;
they are like the morning grass,
[6] which springs up new at dawn,
and withers dry by evening.
[7] We are destroyed by your anger
and terrified by your wrath.
[8] You exposed our sins before you,
our secret sins in the light of your face.
[9] All our days pass under your wrath;
we finish our years with a cry of pain.

My years are of little importance in your sight, O Lord, but to me they are wonderful and mysterious, for my end is known only to you. You created all things and from dust you made me and my fathers before me; they have passed away like the night, and one day my body also will rest in the dust. But your life goes on eternally, O God, and I commend my living soul into your hands. Abide with me at the time of my passing. Amen.

30 JULY

Each morning grant us your faithful love

PSALM 90:10-17

[10] Our span of life is seventy years,
    or eighty if we have the strength,
but all that time is worry and trouble;
    they quickly pass, and we fly away.
[11] Who feels the power of your anger?
    Your wrath is as great
    as the fear you are due.
[12] Teach us to count our days,
    that we may gain a wise heart.
[13] O Yahweh, return! How long must we wait?
    Have pity on your servants.
[14] Each morning grant us your faithful love,
    that we may sing for joy
    and be glad all our days.
[15] May our joy be as long
    as the time you afflicted us,
    the years when we knew disaster.
[16] May your marvels be known to your servants,
    and your glory to their children.
[17] May the favour of the Lord our God
    rest on us;
establish the work of our hands for us,
establish the work of our hands!

As my years grow, teach me your wisdom, Lord, for I am but a child in the ways of the spirit. No one knows the length of his (or her) years, but you know all that life holds in store. May I walk with you each day in faithfulness and love. Fill me with joy at the marvels of your creation. Establish me in your righteousness, O God, and abide with me always. Amen.

31 JULY

My God whom I trust

PSALM 91:1-8

[1] Whoever lives in the the shelter of the Most High,
and dwells under the Almighty's shadow,
[2] will say of Yahweh:
"My refuge and fortress,
my God whom I trust."
[3] He will save you from the fowler's snare,
from deadly plague.
[4] He covers you with his feathers
and beneath his wings you find a refuge;
his faithful love is shield and armour.
[5] You will not fear the terror of night,
nor the arrow that flies by day,
[6] the pestilence that stalks in darkness,
the plague that strikes at noon.
[7] A thousand may fall at your side,
ten thousand to your right,
but you will be unscathed.
[8] You have only to look to see,
the payment received by the wicked.

Shelter me under your invisible wings, Lord, and be my refuge and my fortress all my life long. May your faithful love be my shield from the wicked arrows that attack me by day and from the terrors that assail me by night. If you are with me, who can defeat me? If you are my guide, how can I fall into trap or snare? From pestilence and plague protect me, O God. Amen.

1 AUGUST

Yahweh will put his angels to guard you

PSALM 91:9-16

[9] If you make Yahweh your safe retreat,
the Most High your dwelling-place,
[10] no disaster shall come on you,
no misfortune approach your tent.
[11] He will put his angels in charge of you,
to guard you wherever you go.
[12] They will hold you up in their arms,
so your feet are not injured by stones.
[13] You can tread on the lion and the adder;
you can trample on the young lion and snake.
[14] "I will save him because he is faithful to me;
I will raise him because he trusts in my name.
[15] When he calls to me, I will answer him;
in times of trouble I shall be with him;
I will rescue and honour him.
[16] With long life I will satisfy him;
and let him see my salvation."

May your angels guard my going out and my coming in, O God, and may your power protect me from evil by day and by night. Watch over the tent of my soul that no disaster or misfortune may come near. Hold me up in times of stress and guide my feet through the difficulties that face me each day. I trust in you, O Lord, for you are my Saviour and my Deliverer. Amen.

2 AUGUST

O Yahweh, how great are your deeds

PSALM 92:1-9

[1] It is good to give thanks to Yahweh,
to sing psalms to your name, O Most High,
[2] to proclaim your faithful love at dawn
and your constancy every night,
[3] to the sound of the ten-stringed lyre
and the music of the harp,
[4] for your deeds bring me joy, O Yahweh;
the work of your hands makes me sing for joy.
[5] O Yahweh, how great are your deeds,
how very deep are your thoughts!
[6] The stupid person does not know,
fools do not understand,
[7] that though the wicked grow like grass
and evil-doers prosper,
they will be destroyed forever.
[8] But you are exalted forever, O Yahweh,
[9] for surely your foes, O Yahweh,
surely your foes will perish;
all evil-doers will be scattered.

I thank you with a full heart, O God, for all your good gifts, but above all for your faithful and constant love for me, and for all my brothers and sisters in the faith. The signs of your presence in the world are wonderful to me. How can I penetrate your thoughts when you are so mysterious and powerful? Yet, I long to know you and to serve you. The foolish may reject your love, but I will praise you forever. Amen.

3 AUGUST

The righteous will flourish like a palm tree

PSALM 92:10-15

[10] You have raised my head high
like the horns of a wild ox;
I am anointed with rich oils.
[11] I looked on my enemies' ruin;
I heard the rout of my wicked foes.
[12] The righteous will flourish like a palm tree,
and grow like a cedar of Lebanon;
[13] planted in the house of Yahweh,
they flourish in the courts of our God.
[14] They still bear fruit in old age,
staying fresh and green.
[15] They proclaim that Yahweh is upright;
he is my rock,
no fault can be found in him.

How can anyone withstand the power of your love and holiness, O God? Your presence is a marvel within me and around me. I am filled with gratitude that you have chosen me to be your servant. I pray for your blessing throughout the course of my life, until the day when my task here is completed. You are my Rock, O Lord, and I praise you. Amen.

4 AUGUST

From all eternity you exist

PSALM 93

[1] Yahweh is king, robed in majesty,
Yahweh wears royal robes,
armed with might.
The world is set firm, it can never be moved.
[2] Your throne was established long ago;
from all eternity you exist.
[3] O Yahweh, the seas have raised their voice,
the seas have lifted their crashing surf.
[4] Mightier than the voice of the seas,
mightier than the sound of the surf,
mighty on high is Yahweh.
[5] Your laws stand firm;
holiness is the beauty of your house,
O Yahweh, for endless days.

You are my King and my Lord and I worship you with all my heart and soul. You have created the universe and hold it in being, and you are the eternal flame of love. The oceans resound with but an echo of your majesty. You are mighty and powerful beyond all our thoughts can imagine. Your holiness is beautiful and pure in your sanctuary. Your days are endless. O God, I praise you with all my being. Amen.

5 AUGUST

How long will the wicked boast?

PSALM 94:1-11

[1] O Yahweh, God of vengeance,
God of vengeance, show yourself!
[2] Rise up, O Judge of the earth,
pay back the arrogant what they deserve.
[3] O Yahweh, how long will the wicked,
how long will the wicked boast?
[4] They pour out their arrogance;
all the evil-doers are boastful.
[5] They crush your people, O Yahweh;
they oppress your own.
[6] They kill the widow and stranger,
and murder the orphan.
[7] They say that Yahweh does not see,
the God of Jacob pays no heed.
[8] Take heed yourselves, you stupid people;
when will you fools grow wise?
[9] Does he who made the ear not hear?
Does he who made the eye not see?
[10] Does he who controls nations
let them go unpunished?
The teacher of all humanity,
is he ignorant himself?
[11] Yahweh knows all human thoughts
are nothing but a puff of wind.

I await your judgement, O Lord, and I pray for justice for the oppressed peoples of the world. Hasten the downfall of the cruel and arrogant, for they make a mockery of your love. I know that you are in the world and that you see all that happens. All human aspirations are but a breath of wind to you, O God. Teach me your wisdom and help me to understand the mystery of your ways. Amen.

6 AUGUST

Yahweh will not abandon his people

PSALM 94:12-15

[12] O Yahweh, the one you instruct is blessed,
the one you teach from your law,
[13] to bring him relief in troubled days,
until a pit is dug for the wicked.
[14] Yahweh will not abandon his people,
nor forsake his inheritance;
[15] verdicts will once more be founded on justice,
followed by all who are honest of heart.

Teach me your ways, O Lord, and I shall endeavour to learn your love and your laws. It is of great comfort to know that you are with me and that the seeds of your wisdom are growing in my understanding. I wait for you each morning as I awake, for I know that you will never abandon your faithful people. Give me an honest heart, O God, and a respect for justice and righteousness. Amen.

7 AUGUST

O Yahweh, your faithful love held me up

PSALM 94:16-23

[16] Who fights for me against the wicked?
Who stands at my side against evil-doers?
[17] If Yahweh had not been my helper,
I would soon have lived in the silent grave.
[18] When I said that my foot was slipping,
O Yahweh, your faithful love held me up.
[19] When troubled thoughts filled my heart,
your comfort filled my soul with joy.
[20] Do you support a corrupt court,
one that makes misery by its laws?
[21] They band together against the just
and execute the innocent.
[22] But Yahweh has been my strong tower,
my God the rock where I can flee.
[23] He will repay them for their sins
and kill them for their wickedness;
Yahweh our God will finish them.

Stand beside me in the time of peril, O Lord, for I am lost without you. Hold me up when I am in danger of falling. When I am troubled, comfort me with your love. Help me to fight injustice and corruption and to defend the innocent, when they are in need. You are my Rock. On you alone do I rely in my time of trial. Abide with me, this day, and always. Amen.

8 AUGUST

Come to the rock of our salvation

Psalm 95:1-5

[1] Come, let us sing for joy to Yahweh,
a triumphal shout
to the rock of our salvation.
[2] Let us come to his face with thanksgiving
and extol him with music and songs.
[3] For Yahweh is a great God,
the King over all the gods;
[4] in his hand are earth's depths,
and the mountain peaks belong to him.
[5] The sea is his, he made it;
he formed the dry land
with his hands.

I praise you mightily, O God, for your creation is wonderful and your saving love is deep within me. I am filled with joy and I want to sing your praises forever, because you are the King of the universe. The continents and the oceans are the work of your hands: the depths of the seas and the mountain peaks are your creation. With my whole heart I worship you. Amen.

9 AUGUST

Hear his voice: "Do not harden your hearts"

Psalm 95:6-11

[6] Come, let us bow down in worship
and kneel before Yahweh our Maker,

[7] for he is our God,
we are his people,
the flock that he shepherds today
if you but hear his voice:
[8] "Do not harden your hearts
as at Meribah,
as you did at Massah
that day in the desert
[9] where your fathers tested and tried me,
even though they had seen what I did.
[10] For forty years that generation angered me,
and I said,
'They are people whose hearts go astray,
who cannot grasp my ways.'
[11] So I swore on oath in my anger,
'they shall never enter my rest!'"

May the whole world worship you, O God, for you are the Creator and Sustainer of all that exists. Bless the faithful of your flock and shepherd them with your love, that they may not go astray. I pray, Lord, that I may walk with you all the days of my life. Grant that I may be able to conquer temptation and sin. Hear my prayer, O Lord. Amen.

10 AUGUST

Declare Yahweh's victory day after day

PSALM 96:1-6

[1] Sing a new song to Yahweh!
Sing to Yahweh, all the earth!
[2] Sing to Yahweh; bless his name!

Declare his victory day after day,
[3] proclaim his glory among the nations,
his wonders to all the peoples!
[4] Yahweh is great, and worth great praise,
more awesome than all the gods.
[5] The gods of the nations are only idols;
it was Yahweh who made the heavens.
[6] Splendour and might are all around him;
power and beauty are in his sanctuary.

The music in my heart reflects your wondrous glory, O Lord, for your ways are marvellous to me. Your glory is almost beyond my imagination, though I see your reflection in your mighty works. I am full of awe as I worship in the sanctuary of the universe you have made. May all the nations of the world be granted a vision of your majesty. Amen.

11 AUGUST

Yahweh comes to judge the world

Psalm 96:7-13

[7] Ascribe to Yahweh, you families of nations,
ascribe to Yahweh the glory and power,
[8] ascribe to Yahweh his name's due glory,
bring a gift and enter his courts;
[9] worship Yahweh in the splendour of holiness,
tremble before him, all the earth!
[10] Declare among the nations, "Yahweh is King!"
The world is set firm and will never be moved;
and he will judge the nations justly.
[11] May the heavens rejoice and earth be glad!

May the seas roar and everything in them!
[12] May the fields exult and all that is in them!
May the trees of the forest all shout for joy
[13] and sing before Yahweh when he comes!
When he comes to judge the world
he will judge the world in righteousness
and the peoples by his truth.

May all nations worship you, O Lord, and may all peoples perceive your glory and power which are all around for everyone to see. You are the King of heaven and earth and by your power alone the universe stands. The whole of nature is your praise, for you are the Creator of all that exists. All you have given to me is yours and to you I return all that I have. I await your coming, O God, and I long for truth and justice to prevail. Amen.

12 AUGUST

In the presence of the Lord of the earth

PSALM 97:1-6

[1] Yahweh reigns! Let earth be glad
and distant isles rejoice!
[2] Clouds and thick darkness enfold him;
he set his throne on justice and judgement;
[3] fire goes ahead of him
burning his foes on every side;
[4] his lightning strikes throughout the world;
the earth sees it and quakes.
[5] In Yahweh's presence
mountains melt like wax,

in the presence of
the Lord of the earth.
[6] The heavens declare his righteousness
and all the nations see his glory.

Out of your mystery, O God, the works of your hands have emerged for the whole world to see. Your kingdom stretches from heaven to earth and your presence within this world is manifest in your glory and power. You will bring righteousness and justice to the nations, and all peoples will behold the glory of your throne. I praise you, O God. Amen.

13 AUGUST

May those who love Yahweh hate evil

PSALM 97:7-12

[7] Those who worship idols
and those who boast of idols
are put to shame.
Worship him, you gods!
[8] Zion hears and rejoices,
the towns of Judah are glad,
to hear your judgements, O Yahweh.
[9] You, O Yahweh, are Most High above earth,
far exalted above all gods.
[10] May those who love Yahweh hate evil,
for he guards the lives of his faithful
and rescues them
from the hand of the wicked.
[11] Light is shed on the just
and joy on the upright of heart.

[12] Rejoice in Yahweh, all you just,
and praise his holy name.

Those who put their trust in false values, Lord, have not apprehended your ways. May all people come to know you and worship you. May all nations rejoice in your glory as gladly as the saints do in your heavenly city. Keep the faithful on the straight path, O God, and rescue them from evil ways. I rejoice in your love and I praise you wholeheartedly. Amen.

14 AUGUST

Yahweh has remembered his constancy

PSALM 98:1-3

[1] Sing a new song to Yahweh,
for he has done marvellous things;
his right hand and his holy arm
have won him victory.
[2] Yahweh has revealed his saving power,
and displayed his justice
to all the nations;
[3] he has remembered his constancy,
his faithful love
for the house of Israel;
the ends of the earth have seen
the saving power of our God.

My heart is singing, Lord, for your deeds are marvellous. Your holiness and your power are irresistible. Your love is never failing and your faithfulness is eternal. May your justice be revealed among the nations of the earth.

May all nations experience your salvation. I worship you with my whole heart and mind, O God, for your glory is eternal. Amen.

15 AUGUST

Yahweh will judge the earth justly

PSALM 98:4-9

[4] Acclaim Yahweh, all the world,
shout for joy and sing!
[5] Play on the harp to Yahweh,
with the harp
and the sound of choirs;
[6] to the sound of trumpet and horn,
shout for joy before Yahweh the King.
[7] Let the sea roar and all that it holds,
the world and all who live in it.
[8] Let the rivers clap their hands,
and the hills sing together
[9] at Yahweh's approach,
for he comes to judge the earth;
he will judge the earth justly
and the nations with equity.

Everyone will praise you, Lord: everyone will sing for joy at your coming. Your kingship is eternal and the whole of heaven and earth are in your care. Even the mountains and the oceans reflect your glory. May your justice come soon, O God, and may all nations know your kingly rule. I praise you in the depths of my soul. Amen.

16 AUGUST

Our God: Holy is he!

PSALM 99:1-5

[1] Yahweh reigns;
the nations tremble.
His throne is the cherubim;
the earth quakes.
[2] Yahweh is great in Zion,
high over all the nations.
[3] Let them extol
your great, your awesome name!
Holy is he!
[4] You are a mighty king
who loves justice;
you have established
equity in Jacob,
all you have done
is just and right.
[5] Exalt Yahweh our God;
bow down at his footstool.
Holy is he!

O my King and my God, I praise your holy name. Your holiness is a mystery and a wonder to me, and yet your love is within me. Your heavenly throne is too wonderful and majestic for the human eye to behold, and yet you have chosen me to be your servant. Your heavenly city is beautiful in my imagination, but in reality it must be more glorious and dazzling than all the suns in the universe. I worship and adore you, Lord. Amen.

17 AUGUST

They called and he answered

PSALM 99:6-9

[6] Moses and Aaron
were priests of his;
Samuel was one
who prayed to him.
They called to Yahweh
and he answered;
[7] he spoke from the pillar of cloud;
they kept his statutes,
the Law he gave them.
[8] O Yahweh our God,
you answered them;
you were a God
who forgave them,
and punished their sins.
[9] Exalt Yahweh our God!
Worship at his holy mountain,
for holy is Yahweh our God!

I thank you, O Lord, for the great leaders of past ages, those whom you called to lead your faithful people. It is wonderful that you spoke to them face to face, and I pray that I may be granted a glimpse of your glory. I am unworthy to be called by you, O God, but I seek your forgiveness for my sins. I will praise your holy name always. Amen.

18 AUGUST

It is God who made us

Psalm 100

[1] Let all the earth
 shout for joy to Yahweh;
[2] serve Yahweh with gladness;
 come into his presence
 with songs of joy.
[3] Know that Yahweh is God;
 it is he who made us and we are his;
 we are his people,
 the sheep of his pasture.
[4] Go through his gates with thanksgiving
 and enter his courts singing praise;
 give thanks to him
 and praise his name.
[5] For Yahweh is good,
 eternal his faithful love;
 his faithfulness lasts
 through all generations.

So wonderful is your glory, O Lord, that everyone on earth should sing for joy. It is a delight when I enter your sanctuary and sing your praises with the community of the faithful. I know you are God and that you created me and the whole of the universe at a thought. I give thanks as I enter your courts: I praise your faithful love which lasts forever. Amen.

19 AUGUST

I will sing of your faithful love

PSALM 101:1-5

[1] I will sing
of your faithful love and justice;
to you, O Yahweh, I will sing.
[2] I will take care to live blamelessly;
when will you come to me?
I will live in my house with an innocent heart;
[3] I shall not look at anything vile.
The hateful work of faithless people
will gain no hold on me.
[4] People of perverted hearts
shall not come near me;
I will have nothing to do with evil.
[5] I silence those who slander neighbours;
I will not endure the proud and arrogant.

How can I bring your love to those who reject you, Lord? I live close to you and try to live blamelessly, but around me people are perverted from the truth and pursue evil ways. How can I reach them with the good news of your glorious being? I pray that you will reveal yourself to them, O God. Touch them with your presence, that they may know your faithful love and justice. Amen.

20 AUGUST

I will choose the faithful of the land

Psalm 101:6-8

[6] I will choose the faithful of the land
to live with me.
Those whose ways are blameless
will be my ministers.
[7] My household will have no treacherous people;
no liars will come where I can see them.
[8] Every dawn I will put to silence
all the wicked in the land,
ridding Yahweh's city of all evil-doers.

I believe that your kingdom is not open to those who do evil, Lord, so I pray that you will protect me from the influence of evil powers. May those around me also turn from their sin and repent, that they may live daily in your kingdom. It will be wonderful to live as if in heaven, with all the faithful praising you with one voice, as each dawn comes. Hear my prayer, O God. Amen.

21 AUGUST

O Yahweh, hear my prayer

Psalm 102:1-12

[1] O Yahweh, hear my prayer;
let my cry for help reach you.
[2] Do not hide your face from me
when I am in trouble.
Turn your ear to me;

when I call, answer quickly.
[3] For my days disappear like smoke;
my bones burn like embers.
[4] My heart is like blighted grass;
I fail to eat my food.
[5] Through my groaning aloud
I am mere skin and bone.
[6] I am like a desert owl,
like an owl screeching in ruins.
[7] I lie awake
like a lone bird on a rooftop.
[8] All day long my enemies taunt me;
those who once praised me now curse with
my name.
[9] I eat ashes as food,
and mix tears with my drink.
[10] In your furious wrath
you have picked me up and discarded me.
[11] My days wane like twilight shadows;
I wither like grass.
[12] But you, O Yahweh, reign forever;
all generations honour you.

In the times when the problems of life are sorely testing me, Lord, hear my prayer and come to my help. Sometimes life seems so pointless and my years are so limited. I suppose at such times I am feeling sorry for myself. Yet I can see there is so much to hope for and there are so many things to be thankful for. I know your reign is eternal, so restore my faith, O God, and answer my call. Amen.

22 AUGUST

Yahweh will hear the plea of the destitute

PSALM 102:13-22

[13] You will arise to show Zion mercy,
for it is time to pity her;
the appointed time has come.
[14] Her stones are dear to your servants;
her very dust moves them to pity.
[15] The nations will fear the name of Yahweh,
and all the kings of the earth your glory.
[16] For Yahweh will rebuild Zion
and appear in his glory.
[17] He will hear the plea of the destitute,
and will not scorn their prayer.
[18] Let this be recorded for a future generation,
for a people not yet born to praise Yahweh:
[19] Yahweh leaned down from the heights of his
sanctuary,
he has looked down from heaven to earth,
[20] to hear the groans of the prisoners
and release those under sentence of death,
[21] to proclaim the name of Yahweh in Zion
and his praise in Jerusalem;
[22] when nations will gather together
and kingdoms to worship Yahweh.

There are so many people in severe circumstances, Lord: some are destitute; some are in prison; some are under sentence of death. Also, some of your faithful servants are persecuted without just cause. Show your compassion upon all who are in need, and give them a vision of your glory. May all the nations come to know you, O

God, and may all people worship you with joy and thanksgiving. Amen.

23 AUGUST

Your servants' children will dwell secure

PSALM 102:23-28

[23] He broke my strength before my life is run;
he has cut short my allotted time.
[24] So I said, "O my God,
do not remove me in the midst of my days;
for your years extend through all generations.
[25] In the beginning you laid the foundations of earth,
the heavens are all the work of your hands.
[26] They will perish, but you remain;
they will all wear out like clothes;
like a garment you will change them,
and they will be discarded.
[27] But you remain the same,
and your years never end.
[28] Your servants' children will dwell secure,
and their descendants will live in your
presence."

I pray, O God, for the grace to accept both good times and difficult times, in the strong faith that your ultimate purpose for me and for the whole of humankind will be fulfilled. The universe is your creation, but even when that comes to an end, you will remain, eternal and unchanging. May the faithful grow in their faith and may their children always live in your presence. Amen.

24 AUGUST

Yahweh forgives all your sins

PSALM 103:1-5

[1] Praise Yahweh, my soul,
I praise his holy name
from the depths of my heart.
[2] Praise Yahweh, my soul,
and never forget his kindnesses.
[3] He forgives all your sins,
and cures all your illnesses;
[4] he saves your life from the pit;
and crowns you with faithful love and mercy;
[5] he satisfies you all your life with goodness,
and renews your youth like an eagle's.

I praise you, O God, for you have renewed me constantly and you have forgiven my transgressions. When I have fallen you have raised me up and when I have been ill you have comforted me. With your Spirit guiding me, my own spirit is always full of strength and vigour. May your faithful love and mercy follow me all the days of my life. Amen.

25 AUGUST

Yahweh is merciful and gracious

PSALM 103:6-14

[6] Yahweh is righteous in all he does,
and just to all the oppressed.
[7] He made his ways known to Moses,
his deeds to the people of Israel.

[8] Yahweh is merciful and gracious,
slow to get angry,
full of faithful love.
[9] He will not be always accusing,
nor nurse his anger forever.
[10] He does not act as our sins deserve,
or give us our due for our offences;
[11] his faithful love for those who fear him
is as high as the heavens above the earth.
[12] As far as the east is from the west,
that far he takes our sins from us.
[13] As a father treats his children tenderly,
so Yahweh is tender to those who fear him.
[14] He knows how we were made
and remembers that we are dust.

Thank you, Lord, for the many witnesses in past times to your mercy and grace. Grant me not what I deserve but, according to your faithful love and forgiveness, heal me and make me whole. You created me, O God, and it is wonderful to know that I am one of your children. Yet, your love is deeper than the love of any human parent, and I know that your tender care is all-embracing for all who turn to you. Amen.

26 AUGUST

Yahweh's eternal faithful love

PSALM 103:15-18

[15] The days of mortals are just like grass,
they flourish like flowers in the fields,
[16] then the gales blow and they disappear
and no one remembers where they grew.

[17] But Yahweh's eternal faithful love
is with those who fear him;
his justice stays with their children's children,
[18] with those who keep his covenant
and obey his precepts with care.

Life on earth is so short, Lord, but yet it can be wonderful when lived in the awareness of your presence. People are like ships that pass in the night, but the ocean of your love is never-ending. Your promise of eternal life for those who love you is wonderful, O God, and I live in that hope. May future generations also come to be part of your covenant and may your love abide with them also. Amen.

27 AUGUST

Praise Yahweh, you angels of his

Psalm 103:19-22

[19] Yahweh has set his throne in heaven;
his kingly power rules the world.
[20] Praise Yahweh, you angels of his,
you mighty ones who do his word!
[21] Praise Yahweh, you heavenly armies,
you who carry out his will!
[22] Praise Yahweh, all his works,
everywhere he rules!
Praise Yahweh, my soul!

With all angels and saints I worship you, O Lord, for you are King of the heavenly realms and ruler of the universe you have created. I thank you for the hosts of angels who do your work, especially for those who watch over every one of your children. I praise you for all your mighty works and I glorify your name with all my heart and soul. I praise you, O God. Amen.

28 AUGUST

My God, how great you are

PSALM 104:1-9

[1] Praise Yahweh, my soul;
O Yahweh my God, how great you are,
clothed in splendour and majesty.
[2] He wraps himself with light like a garment;
he spreads the heavens like a tent,
[3] and builds his palace on the waters;
he makes the clouds his chariot
and rides on the wings of the wind.
[4] Winds are his messengers
and flames of fire his servants.
[5] He fixed the earth on its foundations,
never to be moved.
[6] You clothed it with the deep like a cloak,
the seas covered the mountains,
[7] but the waters fled at your command,
they took to flight when you thundered,
[8] and flowed across mountains, down the valleys
and into the place you assigned to them.
[9] You fixed a limit they could not pass;
never again will they flood the earth.

I praise you, O Lord, for all the wonders of the universe you have created. I perceive your presence in the beauties of the heavens and in the depths of the oceans. All the elements are at your command and you hold the earth and the seas in their appointed places. Day and night I praise you for the majesty of your glory, which is signed on the whole of creation. Amen.

29 AUGUST

Yahweh provides wine, oil and bread

PSALM 104:10-18

[10] He makes springs gush as waterfalls
which flow between the mountains.
[11] They water all the wild beasts;
the wild donkeys quench their thirst.
[12] Birds of the air nest by the waters
and sing among the bushes.
[13] He waters the mountains from his high dwelling;
by his works he provides
for all that earth needs.
[14] He provides the grass for cattle,
and plants for people to grow,
bringing food from the earth,
[15] wine to gladden people's hearts,
oil to make their faces glow,
and bread to feed their hearts.
[16] The trees of Yahweh flourish,
the Lebanese cedars he planted,
[17] where the birds build their nests
and the stork builds its home in the pines.
[18] The wild goats have the mountains
and rocks are a refuge for badgers.

I thank you, O Lord, for the riches of creation. I praise you for the sunshine and the rain and for the fertile earth. I praise you for the corn and the oil and the wine which gladden my heart. I thank you for all trees and plants and for all animals and birds and fishes. I pray that humans may learn how to care for your creation in all its wonderful variety. O God, hear my prayer and accept my praise. Amen.

30 AUGUST

Yahweh, your works are countless

Psalm 104:19-26

[19] The moon marks the seasons
and the sun knows when to set;
[20] you make the darkness of night
when the beasts of the forest prowl,
[21] and young lions roar for prey,
asking God for their food.
[22] The sun rises
and they slink away
to return to their dens and sleep.
[23] Then people go out to work
and labour until nightfall.
[24] O Yahweh, your works are countless,
you made them all by your wisdom
and filled the earth with creatures.
[25] The vast expanses of the sea
teem with countless creatures,
living things both great and small.
[26] Ships sail on many courses,
and Leviathan, which you made for sport.

Time and space are wonderful boundaries for your creation, Lord, and I praise you for days and nights and for the seasons of the year. For the satisfaction of daily labour and for leisure activities I give you thanks. The marvels of your creation are innumerable, and I praise you for the earth and the sea and the sky and all the variety of creatures they contain. I glorify your name, O God.

31 AUGUST

Renew the face of the earth

PSALM 104:27-30

[27] All these look to you for food
  at the times when they need it.
[28] You provide it and they gather it;
  you open your hand
  to fill them with good things.
[29] If you hide your face
  they are terrified;
when you withhold their breath,
  they die and go back to dust.
[30] When you send your spirit life begins,
  and you renew the face of the earth.

For the abundant providence of your creation, I praise you, O God. I thank you for daily food and for all your daily care. Your open-handed generosity is a marvel and I praise the richness and variety of your gifts to me. For the gift of life I give thanks and for the spirit which pulses within me I give you praise. For the renewal of each day, I glorify your holy name, O God. Amen.

1 SEPTEMBER

I will sing praise to my God

PSALM 104:31-35

[31] May Yahweh's glory last forever;
may Yahweh be pleased with his work.
[32] When he looks at the earth it trembles;
his touch makes the mountains smoke.
[33] I will sing to Yahweh all my life;
as long as I live
I will sing praise to my God.
[34] May my meditation please him
as I rejoice in Yahweh.
[35] But let sinners vanish from earth
and the wicked cease to exist.
Praise Yahweh, my soul!
Praise Yahweh!

My heart is filled with songs of praise, Lord, when I think of all the wonders of the universe. My whole life long I will praise you and thank you for the gift and wonder of living in the knowledge of your glory. May my every thought be pleasing to you, O God, and may my sins be forgiven. Hear my prayer. Amen.

2 SEPTEMBER

He is Yahweh, our God

PSALM 105:1-7

[1] Give thanks to Yahweh, call on his name;
tell the nations what he has done.

[2] Sing to him; make music for him;
tell of all his wonderful deeds.
[3] Glory in his holy name;
let those who seek Yahweh be joyful of heart.
[4] Seek Yahweh and be strong;
always seek his face.
[5] Remember the deeds he has done,
his wonders, the judgements he has delivered.
[6] You stock of Abraham, his servant;
you children of Jacob, his choice:
[7] he is Yahweh, our God;
his judgements fill the earth.

I thank you, O Lord, for the long history of your revelation to humankind and for those spiritual ancestors who answered your call. They showed later generations that those who seek you will receive strength and spiritual power. Your holy name is glorious and your mighty deeds are recorded for all to know. May your justice reign upon earth. Hear my prayer, O God. Amen.

3 SEPTEMBER

He keeps his covenant forever

Psalm 105:8-15

[8] He keeps his covenant forever,
the word he commanded
for a thousand generations,
[9] which he made with Abraham,
the oath he swore to Isaac.
[10] He confirmed it to Jacob as a law,
an eternal covenant with Israel,

[11] saying, "I give you a land,
Canaan, the share you inherit."
[12] When they were small in number,
few, and strangers in the land,
[13] roaming from nation to nation,
from one kingdom to another,
[14] he allowed no one to oppress them.
He gave orders to kings for their sake,
[15] "Do not touch my anointed ones;
do my prophets no harm!"

I praise you for the everlasting covenant you have made with all of creation, Lord; I especially praise you for the ancient mediators of that covenant whose lives are recorded in your revealed word. For the continuing traditions of the faith over countless generations, I am full of praise and thanksgiving; for I, too, am called to be a member of your covenant people. Watch over the faithful, O God, and grant them your blessing. Amen.

4 SEPTEMBER

Yahweh's word proved Joseph right

PSALM 105:16-22

[16] He created a famine in the land,
he destroyed all their food supply;
[17] but he sent a man ahead of them,
Joseph, sold as a slave.
[18] His feet were bruised with shackles,
his neck was put in irons,
[19] until his prediction came true,
and Yahweh's word proved him right.

[20] The king sent orders to free him,
the ruler of nations released him,
[21] and put him in charge of his palace,
supreme over all he possessed,
[22] with power to punish his princes
and teach his counsellors wisdom.

I thank you, O Lord, for providing for all my daily needs. I ask your blessing on those who do not have sufficient money or food; and I pray that the rich nations of the world may learn to share their produce and their skills with the poorer nations. Also, I ask for your guidance and help in fulfilling the responsibilities that you have assigned to me. Hear my prayer, O God. Amen.

5 SEPTEMBER

Yahweh made his people great in number

PSALM 105:23-38

[23] Then Israel went to Egypt;
Jacob settled in the land of Ham.
[24] He made his people great in number,
and made them stronger than their foes,
[25] whose hearts he turned against his people
to double-dealing with his servants.
[26] He sent his servant Moses,
and Aaron whom he had chosen,
[27] to do miraculous deeds among them,
wonders in the land of Ham.
[28] He sent darkness, and all was dark,
but still they defied his commands;

[29] he turned their rivers into blood,
and caused their fish to die.
[30] Their land teemed with frogs,
even in the royal rooms;
[31] at his word came swarms of flies
and gnats throughout their land.
[32] He gave them hail for rain
and lightning flashing everywhere;
[33] he blasted their vines and fig trees,
and shattered the country's trees.
[34] Locusts came at his command,
and numberless grasshoppers,
[35] which ate every blade of green
and devoured all that the soil had grown.
[36] Then he struck all the land's first-born,
the pride of all their manhood,
[37] and brought out Israel
bearing silver and gold;
in all their tribes
there was none who stumbled.
[38] Egypt was glad when they left,
for terror of Israel had seized them.

I thank you, O God, for all the miracles and wonders of this life. For your power in creation and for your control of the forces of nature, I praise you. May all the nations learn to respect your creative power and may they worship you in an awareness of your majesty and glory. For those who are suffering the cruelties of an unjust regime, O Lord, I pray your help and salvation. Amen.

6 SEPTEMBER

He fulfilled his holy word

PSALM 105:39-45

[39] He spread out a cloud to conceal them,
and fire to lighten the night.
[40] When they asked, he sent quails,
and abundance of bread from heaven;
[41] he opened a rock and water gushed out,
and flowed in dry ground as a river.
[42] He fulfilled his holy word
which he gave to his servant Abraham,
[43] he brought out his people rejoicing,
his holy ones with shouts of joy.
[44] He gave them the lands of nations:
they reaped the fruits of others' toil,
[45] in order to keep his statutes
and stay obedient to his laws.
Praise Yahweh!

I rejoice in the abundance of your provision in nature, O Lord, and I give you thanks for all your loving care of your faithful people. The mystery of your presence is wonderful to me and I am full of awe and reverence at the thought of your marvellous power. I praise you for the gift of your holy word in scripture and for your glorious revelation. I praise you mightily, O Lord. Amen.

7 SEPTEMBER

For the sake of his name Yahweh saved them

Psalm 106:1-12

[1] Praise Yahweh!
Give thanks to Yahweh, for he is good;
his faithful love will last forever.
[2] Who can proclaim all Yahweh's triumphs,
or fully voice his praise?
[3] Blessed are they who maintain justice
and do what is right at all times.
[4] O Yahweh, remember me
when you bless your people,
come to my help when you save them,
[5] that I may know the wealth of your chosen,
that I may join in the joy of your nation,
and give praise with your heritage.
[6] We have sinned just like our ancestors,
we have done wicked things, guilty acts.
[7] When our ancestors were in Egypt,
they set no store by your miracles;
they forgot your acts of faithful love,
and defied you by the sea, the Red Sea.
[8] Yet for the sake of his name he saved them,
to make his mighty power known.
[9] The Red Sea dried up when he rebuked it;
he led them through depths turned into a desert.
[10] He saved them from the power of the foe
and rescued them from the enemy's hand.
[11] The waters drowned their enemies;
not one of them survived.
[12] Then they believed what he had said
and sang his praise.

I praise you for your faithful love, O God, and I wish to glorify your holy name always. I pray that all the leaders of the nations may promote justice and righteousness; and I ask your abundant blessing upon all peoples. For my past wrongdoings I seek your gracious forgiveness, Lord, and I pray that your saving power will come upon me. I will sing of your salvation forever. Amen.

8 SEPTEMBER

But they forgot the God who saved them

PSALM 106:13-33

[13] But they soon forgot his deeds
and did not wait for his plans;
[14] they gave in to greed in the wilderness
and challenged God in the desert.
[15] So he gave them what they wanted,
but also sent a wasting sickness.
[16] In the camp they were jealous of Moses,
and of Aaron, the holy one of Yahweh;
[17] so the earth opened and swallowed Dathan,
and buried the people led by Abiram.
[18] Fire broke out among them
and flames consumed the wicked.
[19] They made a calf at Horeb
and worshipped an idol of metal;
[20] they exchanged their Glory
for a cast of a bull, a grass-eating ox;
[21] they forgot the God who saved them,
who had done great deeds in Egypt,
[22] marvels in the land of Ham
and awesome deeds at the Red Sea.

[23] So he said he would destroy them,
but Moses, his chosen,
stood and confronted him,
to turn his wrath from killing them.
[24] Then they rejected the pleasant land,
and did not believe his promises;
[25] they complained in their tents
and would not listen to Yahweh;
[26] so he swore a solemn oath,
to kill them in the desert,
[27] and scatter their offspring
among the nations of many lands.
[28] Then they bound themselves
to the Ba'al of Peor,
and sacrificed to lifeless gods;
[29] their wicked deeds moved Yahweh to anger
and a plague broke out among them.
[30] But Phineas stood and intervened,
and the plague was stopped;
[31] thus he is famed for righteousness
from age to age forever.
[32] They angered Yahweh by the waters of Meribah,
and Moses suffered on their account
[33] for they embittered his spirit
and rash words came from his lips.

I pray that I may always remember your loving grace and constant care, O God. For the many times you have saved me from following false values, and for the many times you have helped me to resist temptation, I give you hearty thanks. Yet I ask your forgiveness once again for the times I have failed you, and I pray that you will abide with me, despite my many shortcomings. Hear my prayer, O Lord. Amen.

9 SEPTEMBER

Yahweh called to mind his covenant

PSALM 106:34-48

[34] They did not destroy the nations
as Yahweh had ordered them,
[35] but associated with them
and adopted their ways.
[36] They worshipped their idols
and found themselves trapped by them;
[37] they offered their sons and their daughters
to demons;
[38] they shed guiltless blood
of their sons and their daughters,
and sacrificed them to the idols of Canaan;
the land was defiled by their blood.
[39] They defiled themselves by their deeds,
for their acts were those of a whore.
[40] Yahweh was furious with his people;
his own heritage disgusted him.
[41] He handed them over
to the power of the nations,
and they were ruled by their foes.
[42] Their enemies oppressed them
and crushed them by their rule.
[43] Many times he saved them,
but they still defied him
and sank ever deeper in sin.
[44] But he pitied their distress
when he heard their cry for help;
[45] he called to mind his covenant;
in faithful love he relented
[46] and caused them to be pitied

by all who held them captive.
[47] O Yahweh, our God, save us,
gather us from among the nations,
that we may thank your holy name
and glory in praising you.
[48] Praise be to Yahweh, the God of Israel,
forever and ever.
Let the people say, "Amen!"
Praise Yahweh!

Save me, O Lord, from accepting the false standards of the world and confirm me in the faith. When I err from the straight path, bring me back into your love; and show the enemies of truth also the way they ought to go. I thank you for your help in past times and I praise you for your eternal and universal covenant. I praise you and I thank you, O God, for all your gracious gifts. Amen.

10 SEPTEMBER

Yahweh saved them from their troubles

PSALM 107:1-9

[1] Give thanks to Yahweh, for he is good;
his faithful love endures forever.
[2] Let those saved by Yahweh say it,
those he saved from the powers of foes,
[3] those he gathered from foreign lands,
from east and west, from north and south.
[4] Some wandered in desert wastes,
finding no road to a peopled city;
[5] hungry and thirsty,
their powers fainted in them.

[6] They cried to Yahweh in their distress,
and he saved them from their troubles;
[7] he led them by a straight road
to a city full of people.
[8] Let them thank Yahweh
for his faithful love
and his wonderful deeds for people;
[9] he provides for the thirsty
and fills the hungry with good things.

I thank you for leading me along the road of life so far, O Lord, and especially I give thanks for your faithful and enduring love. In those times when I have been lost in a wilderness of the spirit, I thank you for leading me into the community of your love. I praise you for your constant and providential care towards those who hunger and thirst after your righteousness. I glorify your name, O God. Amen.

11 SEPTEMBER

Let them thank Yahweh

PSALM 107:10-32

[10] Some sat in darkness and gloom,
miserably fettered in chains,
[11] for they had disobeyed God
and defied the plan of the Most High.
[12] Their hearts were crushed by hard labour;
when they fell there was none to help.
[13] They cried to Yahweh in their distress,
and he saved them from their troubles;
[14] he brought them from darkness

and the shadow of death,
and struck off their chains.
[15] Let them thank Yahweh
for his faithful love,
and his wonderful deeds for people,
[16] for he breaks down gates of bronze
and smashes bars of iron.
[17] Rebellion turned some into fools,
made wretched for their sins;
[18] they loathed all sight of food,
they came to the gates of death.
[19] They cried to Yahweh in their distress,
and he saved them from their troubles.
[20] He sent his word to heal them,
and saved them from the grave.
[21] Let them thank Yahweh
for his faithful love,
and his wonderful deeds for people.
[22] Let them give thank-offerings,
and tell of his deeds with shouts of joy.
[23] Some went out to sea in ships,
as traders on great oceans;
[24] they saw the works of Yahweh,
his wonderful deeds in the deep;
[25] by his word he raised the storms
that lifted high the waves.
[26] Thrown to the sky and into the depths,
their courage melted in distress;
[27] they reeled about like drunkards,
and all their skills were useless.
[28] They cried to Yahweh in their distress,
and he saved them from their troubles;
[29] the storm sank to a breath;

the waves of the sea were stilled.
[30] They rejoiced at the calm
and he brought them safe to their harbour.
[31] Let them thank Yahweh
for his faithful love,
and his wonderful deeds for people.
[32] Let them tell of his greatness
in the people's assembly,
and praise him in the council of elders.

For releasing me from the bondage of sin and death, I thank you, O Lord. For leading me from darkness into the glorious light of your love, I praise you. For your healing power within my soul, I glorify your holy name. I pray that you will guide me out of troubled waters, when I am assailed by the storms of life; and I live in the hope that you will bring me to a safe harbour in your heavenly city. May the whole world know of your glorious love and power. Amen.

12 SEPTEMBER

Think of the faithful love of Yahweh

PSALM 107:33-43

[33] He turns rivers to desert
and gushing springs into arid ground,
[34] fruitful ground becomes salty marsh,
because of the evil of those who lived there.
[35] He turns a desert to pools of water,
and arid ground into gushing springs;
[36] he brings the hungry to live there,
and they build a city to live in.

[37] They plant fields and make vineyards
and gather harvests of their fruits.
[38] He blesses them and their numbers increase;
he keeps their herds full of cattle.
[39] Their numbers decline and they dwindle away
through hardship, disaster and sorrow.
[40] He pours contempt on princes
and makes them wander in trackless wastes;
[41] but he lifts the poor from their distress
and increases their children and flocks.
[42] The upright rejoice at the sight,
and the wicked can say nothing.
[43] If you are wise, take all this to heart,
and think of the faithful love of Yahweh.

For the richness and abundance of your creation, Lord, I give thanks. I pray that the stream of living water which flows from you into the universe may fill my soul with your love and your peace. Grant rich harvests to poor peoples and bless the needy with your providential gifts. May those who follow you rejoice at your word, and may the unbelieving come to know your faithful love. Hear my prayer, O Lord. Amen.

13 SEPTEMBER

Be exalted, God, above the heavens

PSALM 108:1-6

[1] O God, my heart is steadfast,
I will sing and make music, with all my soul.
[2] Awake, lute and harp! I will awaken the dawn.
[3] I will thank you, O Yahweh, with the peoples;

I will sing your praise with the nations;
[4] for your mercy is higher than the heavens,
and your faithful love reaches the skies.
[5] Be exalted, God, above the heavens,
your glory above all the earth.
[6] Save by your might and answer me,
that those you love may be saved.

Make me firm in my faith, Lord, and fill my soul with the music of your holiness and love. I will sing forever of your mercy and grace, for you have brought me into your house and given me a place at your table. May your name be exalted above the skies and may your glory illuminate the whole earth. For your wonderful and saving love, O God, I give you thanks and praise. Amen.

14 SEPTEMBER

Through God we shall fight courageously

PSALM 108:7-13

[7] God has spoken from his sanctuary:
"I will share out Shechem in triumph,
and measure off the Vale of Succoth.
[8] Gilead is mine and Manasseh is mine;
[9] Ephraim, my helmet; my sceptre, Judah;
my washbowl, Moab;
upon Edom I will toss my sandals,
I shout in triumph at Philistia."
[10] Who will lead me to the fortified city?
Who will guide me into Edom?
[11] Only you, who have rejected us.
You march no more, O God, with our ranks.

[12] Grant us help against the foe;
for human help is vain.
[13] Through God we shall fight courageously,
for he will trample down our foes.

Give me the strength and courage, O Lord, to fight for the side of good and to be faithful to my calling in all circumstances. All the nations of the earth belong to you and only in you will they prosper. Likewise, only through your gracious help will I be able to have the victory over the power of Satan. Stand beside me, O God, and give me determination and purpose. Amen.

15 SEPTEMBER

They repay my goodness with evil

PSALM 109:1-20

[1] O God, whom I praise, do not keep silent,
[2] for wicked and lying mouths are open,
speaking lying words against me.
[3] They surround me with words of hatred
and attack me without a cause.
[4] In return for my friendship
they denounce me,
but I continue to pray.
[5] They repay my goodness with evil
and my friendship with hatred.
[6] Set an evil one against them,
let an accuser bring them to trial;
[7] when they are tried,
may they be found guilty,
and may their prayers condemn them.

[8] May their days be few,
and others replace them as leaders.
[9] May their children be orphaned
and their wives widowed.
[10] May their children be homeless beggars
driven from ruined homes.
[11] May creditors seize all they own,
and strangers loot their work.
[12] May no one show faithful love to them,
or pity their orphaned children.
[13] May their offspring die
and their names be forgotten.
[14] May their ancestors' sins
be brought before Yahweh,
and their mothers' sins
never be forgotten.
[15] May their sins always remain before Yahweh,
that he may cut off their memory from earth.
[16] For they never thought to show faithful love,
but drove the poor to death,
the weak and broken-hearted.
[17] They loved to curse others;
may their curses come on them.
They never liked to bless;
may blessings be far away from them.
[18] Cursing for them was like clothes,
it belonged to them like the water they drank,
like the marrow in their bones.
[19] May it wrap them round like a cloak,
like a belt forever tied round them.
[20] May Yahweh repay my accusers like this,
those who speak evil of me.

Protect me from all powers hostile to you, O Lord, and help me to defeat temptation and sin. If those around me repay goodness with evil, I commend them into your care, and I pray for the grace to forgive and to be at peace within myself. May those who behave cruelly and selfishly be brought to see the light of your justice. Hear my prayer, O Lord. Amen.

16 SEPTEMBER

Help me, O Yahweh my God

PSALM 109:21-29

[21] But you, O Yahweh my King,
deal well with me for the sake of your name;
by the goodness of your faithful love,
deliver me;
[22] for I am poor and weak,
and my wounds go right to the heart;
[23] I fade away like shadows at dusk;
I am shaken off like a locust.
[24] My knees give way through fasting;
my body is thin and haggard.
[25] I am put to scorn by my accusers;
they shake their heads when they see me.
[26] Help me, O Yahweh my God;
save me by your faithful love,
[27] and let them know it is by your power,
that you, O Yahweh, have done it.
[28] Let them curse, for you will bless!
Let them attack; they will be put to shame,
and your servant will rejoice!
[29] My accusers will be clothed with disgrace
and be wrapped in shame like a cloak.

In my human weakness and frailty, O God, I ask you to have mercy upon me. Save me from those enemies who attack me, both from within and from without. Help me and save me by the power of your faithful love. May the unrighteous come to know your power and love, and may they be put to shame by your wonderful blessing. Hear my prayer, O Lord. Amen.

17 SEPTEMBER

Yahweh stands in support of the weak

PSALM 109:30-31

[30] I will lift up my voice in thanksgiving to Yahweh;
and praise him in the midst of crowds;
[31] for he stands in support of the weak,
to save their lives from those who condemn them.

I pray for those who are oppressed, Lord, and for those who are wrongly condemned for crimes they have not committed. May all nations come to know your standards of justice and righteousness, and may your love prevail throughout the world. I praise you with heart and soul, O God, for your ways are wonderful to me. Amen.

18 SEPTEMBER

Sit at my right hand

PSALM 110:1-3

[1] Yahweh declared to my lord,
"Sit at my right hand

until I have made
your foes a footstool for your feet."
[2] Yahweh will stretch out your sceptre from Zion
so that you may rule
over all your foes.
[3] Your people pay homage
on the day you lead out your armies
arrayed in holiness.
From the womb of the dawn,
you have the dew of your youth.

I pray, O God, that all earthly rulers may pay homage to you, the King of all kings and Lord of all earthly lords. May all peoples acknowledge your rule over both heaven and earth, and may they order their lives in accord with your will. May all your enemies be overcome by your love; and may they worship the beauty of your holiness, now and for evermore. Amen.

19 SEPTEMBER

You are a priest forever

PSALM 110:4-7

[4] Yahweh has sworn and will never retract,
"You are a priest forever
in the line of Melchisedek."
[5] At your right hand
the Lord will bring down kings
on the day of his fury.
[6] He will judge the nations,
heaping up their dead;
he will bring down the rulers

of the whole earth.
[7] He will drink at the torrent on the way;
and so he will hold his head high.

Bless those who have dedicated themselves to your service, O God, in whatever capacity they have done so. Help them to be faithful to their vows, as you are faithful to your covenant. May your judgement fall on those who rule irresponsibly, but may those who follow righteousness have your help in all their designs. Hear my prayer, O Lord. Amen.

20 SEPTEMBER

Yahweh has won renown for his marvellous deeds

PSALM 111:1-5

[1] Praise Yahweh!
With all my heart I will give thanks to Yahweh,
in the congregation,
in the assembly of the righteous.
[2] Great are the deeds of Yahweh,
they are weighed by all
who delight in him.
[3] His deeds are full of splendour and majesty;
his justice remains firm forever.
[4] He has won renown for his marvellous deeds,
Yahweh is gracious and tender.
[5] He meets the needs of all those who fear him,
he keeps his covenant forever.

I praise you and I worship you, O Lord, with all my heart and soul. I love to worship you with the community of the faithful, because your acts of creation and your mighty deeds are celebrated with such joy. Your love is more wonderful than any human love and your care for those who follow you is inspiring. I will praise you all my days. Amen.

21 SEPTEMBER

The root of wisdom is fear of Yahweh

PSALM 111:6-10

[6] He has shown his people the power of his works,
by giving them the lands of the nations.
[7] All that he does is faithful and just;
his precepts are founded on justice.
[8] They will stand forever and ever,
achieved in constancy and truth.
[9] He sent and redeemed his people;
he imposed his covenant forever;
his name is holy, inspiring awe.
[10] The root of wisdom is fear of Yahweh;
all who live by it
grow in wisdom.
His praise will continue forever.

I pray for wisdom in your ways, O Lord, and I seek to live according to your law of love. I have beheld the wonder of your mighty works and I stand in awe before your throne of grace. Your word is eternal, O God, and all truth lies in your heavenly wisdom. The whole world will praise your holy name forever. Amen.

22 SEPTEMBER

Blessed the one who fears Yahweh

PSALM 112:1-4

[1] Praise Yahweh!
Blessed the one who fears Yahweh,
who finds delight in his commands.
[2] The children will be great in the land,
an upright race forever blessed.
[3] The house will be full of blessings and wealth,
where righteousness endures forever.
[4] Even in darkness light shines for the upright,
for the gracious, compassionate and good.

I ask for your blessing each day, O Lord, and I pray for your guidance. My heart is full of both reverence and delight when I consider your holiness and love. Bless also the community in which I live and give the families of the faithful prosperity and happiness. Your light shines into the darkest corners of life, O God, and I pray that you will illuminate my days with your compassion and goodness. Amen.

23 SEPTEMBER

Remembered forever for righteousness

PSALM 112:5-10

[5] Good comes to one who is gracious in lending,
whose business is managed with justice.
[6] Surely such will never be shaken,
remembered forever for righteousness.

[7] Bad news will bring no fear
to a steadfast heart that trusts Yahweh.
[8] A steadfast heart need never fear,
for all things end in triumph over foes.
[9] The poor who gain from lavish gifts,
bring good renown that never fades,
and dignity held high in honour.
[10] The wicked will see it with angry eyes
and gnash their teeth and waste away;
for wicked longings come to nought.

May all my dealings be fair and just, Lord, in the light of your presence. If your righteousness touches me, then I shall not be afraid of bad times. Give me a steadfast heart, free from wicked thoughts. Remove all jealous or envious designs from my mind and may my prayers and actions support those who are less fortunate than myself. Hear my prayer, O Lord. Amen.

24 SEPTEMBER

Let Yahweh's name be blessed

PSALM 113:1-6

[1] Praise Yahweh!
Praise Yahweh, you his servants,
praise the name of Yahweh.
[2] Let Yahweh's name be blessed
both now and forever.
[3] From dawn to sunset
let Yahweh's name be praised.
[4] Supreme is Yahweh, over all nations,
and his glory over the heavens.

[5] Who can compare with Yahweh, our God?
His throne stands on high,
[6] but he stoops to regard both heaven and earth.

I praise you, O God, because you are glorious on your heavenly throne, but yet you watch over each of your children with love and care. I will sing your praises all day long, for you are King of the universe and Lord of heaven. I glorify your holy name because you have allowed me to have a glimpse of the wonders of your creation. I praise you for all your gracious acts and for your unfailing love. Amen.

25 SEPTEMBER

Yahweh lifts the weak and raises the poor

PSALM 113:7-9

[7] He lifts the weak from the dust
and raises the poor from the ashes,
[8] to seat them with princes,
with his people's princes.
[9] He gives the barren woman a home
as a happy mother of children.
Praise Yahweh!

I pray, O God, that the inequalities of life may be set right by your just actions. May the poor and weak know your special grace; and may the rich and privileged show compassion on those less fortunate than themselves. I pray for the lonely, and especially for those not blessed with children. May they know your love in deep measure. Hear my prayer, O Lord. Amen.

26 SEPTEMBER

Quake, earth, in the Lord's presence

PSALM 114

[1] When Israel escaped from Egypt,
and the house of Jacob
from people of a strange language,
[2] Judah became God's sanctuary
and Israel his domain.
[3] The sea looked and fled,
the River Jordan turned back,
[4] the mountains skipped like goats
and the hills like lambs.
[5] Sea, what made you flee?
Jordan, why did you turn back?
[6] Mountains, why did you skip,
and hills, why were you like lambs?
[7] Quake, earth, in the Lord's presence,
in the presence of the God of Jacob,
[8] who turned the rock into a pool,
hard rock into springs of water.

For your providential care and special grace, Lord, I thank you. For those times when you have revealed to me glimpses of your glory, I praise your holy name. I know your presence deep within, but I also perceive your glory in the wondrous things you have created. For revealing yourself in past ages by your mighty deeds, I praise you. I thank you also for your revelations to humankind through the scriptures. I praise and thank you, O God. Amen.

27 SEPTEMBER

Our God does whatever he wills

PSALM 115:1-8

[1] Do not ascribe the glory to us, not us,
but to your name, O Yahweh,
because of your faithful and constant love.
[2] Why do the nations ask,
"Where is their God?"
[3] Our God is in heaven,
and he does whatever he wills.
[4] Their idols are made of silver and gold,
fashioned by human skill;
[5] they have mouths but cannot speak;
they have eyes but cannot see;
[6] they have ears but cannot hear;
they have noses but cannot smell;
[7] they have hands but cannot feel;
they have feet but cannot walk;
they cannot utter a sound from their throats.
[8] Those who make them are just like them,
and so are all who trust in them.

I put my trust in you, Lord, for you are the living God who rules over heaven and earth. To you alone are the glory and the power and the majesty, which are due to your holiness and all-encompassing love. When I meditate on your ways I become aware of my dependence on your grace, yet I know that you love each and every one of your children. I praise you and I thank you, O God. Amen.

28 SEPTEMBER

Yahweh will keep us in mind

PSALM 115:9-13

[9] House of Israel, trust in Yahweh,
he is their help and shield;
[10] House of Aaron, trust in Yahweh,
he is their help and shield.
[11] You who fear him, trust in Yahweh,
he is their help and shield.
[12] Yahweh will keep us in mind, to bless us;
he will bless the House of Israel;
he will bless the House of Aaron.
[13] He will bless all who fear Yahweh,
small and great alike.

Be my help and shield in all the chances and changes of my life, O God. I place my trust in you, for you alone are the Lord of life. May the whole community be protected by your power and may all who believe in you be confirmed in their faith. Keep me in mind, especially at those times when life is busy and full of cares. Hear my prayer, O Lord. Amen.

29 SEPTEMBER

We are the ones who extol Yahweh

PSALM 115:14-18

[14] May Yahweh add to your numbers,
both you and your children;
[15] may you be blessed by Yahweh,
maker of heaven and earth.

[16] Yahweh owns the highest heavens,
but he gave the earth to the human race.
[17] The dead cannot praise Yahweh,
those who descend into silence;
[18] we are the ones who extol Yahweh,
both now and for eternity.
Praise Yahweh!

O God, Maker of heaven and earth, give your abundant blessing to those who praise you. My heart is full of gratitude for the wonders of this world that you have allotted to your creatures. I pray that all human beings may learn a sense of responsibility for the environment in which you have placed them. May all nations also come to praise you for the beauty and richness of this world, your gift. Amen.

30 SEPTEMBER

Yahweh saves the simple-hearted

PSALM 116:1-6

[1] I love Yahweh, for he hears me,
and listens to my prayer.
[2] Because he turned his ear to me,
I call on him
through all my days.
[3] The bonds of death closed in on me;
the snares of the grave bound me tight;
pain and torment held me fast.
[4] I invoke Yahweh by name:
"I implore you,
save me, O Yahweh."

[5] Yahweh is graceful and righteous;
our God is full of compassion.
[6] Yahweh saves the simple-hearted;
when I was low he gave me strength.

I love you with my whole heart, O Lord, for you are full of compassion and forgiveness. In past times you have answered my cry for help. When I have been in danger, you have saved me. The marvel of your gracious love is written on my soul. May the simplicity of my faith be acceptable to you, this day and always. Amen.

1 OCTOBER

I shall walk before Yahweh

PSALM 116:7-11

[7] Return, my heart, to peace again,
 for Yahweh has delivered you.
[8] You have saved me from death,
 my eyes from tears,
 my feet from tripping;
[9] I shall walk before Yahweh in the land of life.
[10] My trust did not fail even as I said,
 "I am bitterly distressed."
[11] In my terror I cried,
 "All people are faithless."

Only in you, Lord, do I put my trust, for you alone are perfect in faithfulness and love. When I have been afraid or in distress I have been able to turn to you for help. Abide with me all through my life, for without you I am a lost soul. Give me peace in my heart and mind, that I may face each day with courage. Hear my prayer, O God. Amen.

2 OCTOBER

I will pay my vows to Yahweh

PSALM 116:12-14

[12] How can I repay all Yahweh does,
 all the gifts he pours on me?
[13] I will lift up the cup of salvation
 to call on the name of Yahweh,

[14] and pay my vows to Yahweh
in the face of all his people.

The abundance of your gifts to me is overwhelming, O God. How can I ever repay you? Even my personal qualities and abilities are gifts from you. I can only, therefore, return to you what is yours already. Will you accept my promise to serve you, in the context of your grace, within the community of the faithful? So I will to do, but only if your will is in mine will I succeed. Hear my prayer, O Lord. Amen.

3 OCTOBER

I will bring a gift of thanksgiving

PSALM 116:15-19

[15] A precious thing in Yahweh's sight
is the death of those who die faithful to him.
[16] Truly, O Yahweh, I am your slave;
I am your slave,
the child of your slave.
You have loosed the fetters that bound me.
[17] To you I will bring a gift of thanksgiving,
and invoke Yahweh by name.
[18] I will pay my vows to Yahweh
in the face of all his people,
[19] in the courts of Yahweh's house,
in the midst of you, Jerusalem.
Praise Yahweh!

My whole life is yours, O God, and until the day I die I would wish to serve you. You have redeemed me from the chains of sin and death, and I give you thanks for my deliverance. In thanksgiving I bring what I have to give to you, the service of my thoughts and deeds and words. May my gift be acceptable in your sight, O God, and may your grace and help support me in my endeavours. Amen.

4 OCTOBER

Extol Yahweh, all you peoples

PSALM 117

[1] Praise Yahweh, all you nations;
extol him, all you peoples.
[2] For great is his faithful love,
and the truth of the Lord lasts forever.
Praise Yahweh.

I thank you, O God, for the truths about yourself and your creation which you have revealed to humankind through your holy scriptures. May all nations and peoples come to praise you and to know your truth; and may that same truth set all peoples free from the bondage of selfishness and sin. The whole universe will praise your faithful love forever. Amen.

5 OCTOBER

It is good to give thanks to Yahweh

PSALM 118:1-9

[1] Praise Yahweh!
It is good to give thanks to Yahweh;
his faithful love is eternal.

[2] Let the house of Israel say,
"His faithful love is eternal";
[3] let the house of Aaron say,
"His faithful love is eternal";
[4] let those who fear Yahweh say,
"His faithful love is eternal".
[5] When I called in distress to Yahweh,
he heard me and set me free.
[6] Yahweh is with me, I will not fear;
what can anyone do to me?
[7] With Yahweh with me as my help,
I gloat over my enemies.
[8] To seek refuge in Yahweh is better
than to trust any person;
[9] to seek refuge in Yahweh is better
than to trust in princes.

I trust in you, O Lord, for your faithful love lasts forever. May all the faithful community come to know of your constancy. In times past you have heard my calls for help and you have saved me from danger and from temptation. If you are with me, whom should I fear, for no one is able to defeat you or change your will. Abide with me forever, Lord. Amen.

6 OCTOBER

My strength and my song is Yahweh

PSALM 118:10-14

[10] All the nations surrounded me;
in Yahweh's name I cut them down.
[11] They surrounded me on every side;

in Yahweh's name I cut them down.
[12] They swarmed around me like bees,
they flared up like a brushwood fire;
in Yahweh's name I cut them down.
[13] I was pushed back, about to fall,
but Yahweh came to my help.
[14] My strength and my song is Yahweh;
he has become my salvation.

Help me to defeat the powers of evil, Lord, and strengthen my right arm to have the victory over those who despise your name. If I should fall, pick me up again that I may renew the good fight in the cause of righteousness. You are my strength and my song each day of my life. You are my salvation and my strong rock. I praise you, O God for your grace and help. Amen.

7 OCTOBER

I will proclaim what Yahweh has done

PSALM 118:15-21

[15] Shouts of joy and salvation
fill the tents of the righteous:
"Yahweh's right hand has done wonders!
[16] Yahweh's right hand is lifted high!
Yahweh's right hand has done wonders!"
[17] I will not die, but live
and proclaim what Yahweh has done.
[18] Yahweh has punished me sternly
but he did not allow me to die.
[19] Open the gates of justice for me;
I will go through and thank Yahweh.

[20] This is the gate of Yahweh
where the upright go in.
[21] I will praise you, for you have answered me,
and made yourself my Saviour.

Those who love you, Lord, are full of joy. I, too, am joyful, because you have given me the gift of life with your love. I have suffered for my past sins, but you have forgiven me and I am made whole again. You have invited me to enter the gates of your kingdom, and I long to be with you forever. For your answers to my prayers, O God, I thank you from the bottom of my heart. Amen.

8 OCTOBER

This is the day that Yahweh has made

PSALM 118:22-29

[22] The stone the builders rejected
has become the cornerstone;
[23] Yahweh has done this,
and it is wonderful to see.
[24] This is the day that Yahweh has made;
let us rejoice and be glad in it.
[25] O Yahweh, we beg you to save us;
O Yahweh, grant us success.
[26] He is blessed who comes in Yahweh's name;
from Yahweh's house we bless you!
[27] Yahweh is God;
he has given us light.
With branches in hand,
form your processions
as far as the horns of the altar.

[28] You are my God and I thank you;
all praise to you, my God.
[29] It is good to give thanks to Yahweh;
his faithful love is eternal.

Each day I rejoice in the new day you have made, O Lord. Once I was lost and rejected, but you found me and showed me your steadfast love. Continue to shine your lamp before me, that I may walk in the straight path. May all the community of the faithful rejoice together in your many blessings. You are my King and my God, and I thank you and praise you for all you have done for me. Amen.

9 OCTOBER

Blessed are they whose path is blameless

PSALM 119:1-8

[1] Blessed are they whose path is blameless,
who walk in the law of Yahweh.
[2] Blessed are they who keep his testimonies
and seek him with their whole heart,
[3] who do no wrong and walk in his ways.
[4] You have laid down precepts
to be carefully kept.
[5] May my course be steady
in keeping your statutes;
[6] I shall not then be shamed
if my eyes are fixed on your commands.
[7] With an honest heart I will thank you
as I learn your righteous judgements.
[8] I will observe your statutes;
do not leave me abandoned.

My imperfections are many, O Lord, but it is wonderful to read your holy word and to know of your law of love. If you guide me, I may grow both in your law and in your love. If my path is towards you, then I shall never need to feel ashamed. I ask for an honest heart and for a spirit willing to do your will. I pray that you will never leave me without your instruction. Hear my prayer, O God. Amen.

10 OCTOBER

I will take delight in your statutes

PSALM 119:9-16

[9] How can a youth tread a pure path?
by living by your word.
[10] I seek you with all my heart,
let me not stray from your commands.
[11] I have hidden your word in my heart
to avoid any sin against you.
[12] You are blessed, O Yahweh,
teach me your statutes.
[13] With my lips I proclaim
all the judgements that come from
your mouth.
[14] I delight in the way of your testimonies
as much as in all kinds of wealth.
[15] I will reflect on your precepts
and fix my eyes on your ways;
[16] I will take delight in your statutes
and I will not forget your word.

I am but a child in your ways, O Lord. I rely upon your help each day, that I may walk in the path by which I ought to go. Your holy word has taken root in my heart and I am always conscious of your presence with me. I love to read your holy word and to learn the riches of your love. I will always delight in your ways, and I pray that you will walk with me. Amen.

11 OCTOBER

Set me free from the scorn and contempt of the proud

PSALM 119:17-24

[17] Be good to your servant
that I may live and keep your word;
[18] open your eyes and show me
the wonders to find in your law.
[19] I am only a traveller on earth,
do not hide your commands from me.
[20] My heart wastes away with longing
at all times for your judgements.
[21] The proud have felt your rebuke,
the cursed who reject your commands;
[22] set me free from their scorn and contempt
for I have obeyed your testimonies.
[23] Though princes sit plotting against me,
your servant reflects on your statutes;
[24] your testimonies are my delight;
I turn to them for counsel.

I hope for your help on my earthly pilgrimage, Lord, for your wisdom exceeds all human knowledge. I desire to serve you all my days and I long to learn more of your revelations. I pray for those who scorn your word, that their eyes may be opened to the truth. Guide me through the maze of sinfulness that surrounds me, and lead me into your glorious kingdom. Amen.

12 OCTOBER

Keep me from deceitful ways

PSALM 119:25-32

[25] My soul clings to the dust;
revive me, as you have promised.
[26] I told you my ways and you answered me;
teach me your statutes.
[27] Show me the way of your precepts
that I may reflect on your wonders.
[28] My soul melts away with grief;
strengthen me, as you have promised.
[29] Keep me from deceitful ways
and grant me the grace of your law.
[30] I have chosen the faithful way;
I set your judgements before me.
[31] O Yahweh, I cling to your testimonies;
do not let me be put to shame.
[32] I run the path of your commands,
for you have set free my heart.

My whole trust is in you, O God. I have confessed my sins and I pray that you will show me the way to follow. I wish to walk in the pathways of righteousness and truth, for then I know that you will be with me. You have freed me from my captivity and I am full of joy that your kingdom is within me. Grant me your grace each day, Lord. Amen.

13 OCTOBER

Turn my eyes from worthless things

PSALM 119:33-40

[33] Teach me the way of your statutes, O Yahweh,
    and I will observe them forever;
[34] give me understanding, I will keep your law
    and observe it with all my heart.
[35] Lead me in the way of your commands,
    for there I find delight.
[36] Bend my heart to your testimonies
    and not to selfish gain;
[37] turn my eyes from worthless things
    and grant me life in your ways.
[38] Keep your promise to your servant,
    so that you may be feared.
[39] Remove the disgrace that I dread,
    for your ordinances are good.
[40] See how I long for your precepts;
    in your justice give me life.

I long with my whole heart to be with you in spirit and truth, O God. Walk with me and teach me your wonderful ways. Help me to grow towards you in all that I endeavour. Keep me from returning to my former selfishness and prevent me from grasping for worthless aims. I find true delight only in trying to do your will; I pray therefore that your will may be in mine. Amen.

14 OCTOBER

I trust in your word

PSALM 119:41-48

[41] Send your faithful love to me, O Yahweh,
    your salvation which you promised;
[42] then I can answer the one who taunts me,
    for I trust in your word.
[43] Do not deny me the word of truth,
    for my hope is in your ordinances,
[44] and I will always keep your law
    forever and ever;
[45] I will walk at liberty,
    for I have sought your precepts.
[46] I will speak to kings of your ordinances,
    and will not be ashamed,
[47] for your commands, which I dearly love,
    fill me with delight.
[48] I revere your commands, which I love,
    and I will reflect on your statutes.

Only in the freedom of your faithful love, O Lord, do I find fulfilment. Grant me the joy of your freedom from falsehood and deceit, and help me to walk in the pathways of truth. I will tell the whole world of your grace and goodness to me, that all may know of the kingdom of your love. I meditate upon your word constantly and it is my guiding star in all that I do. I praise you, O God. Amen.

15 OCTOBER

Your promise gives me life

PSALM 119:49-56

[49] Remember your word to your servant,
in which you have made me hope.
[50] This is my comfort in trouble,
that your promise gives me life.
[51] The arrogant utterly jeer at me
but I do not turn from your law.
[52] When I think of your judgements of old,
O Yahweh, I take comfort.
[53] I am gripped by fury when I see the wicked
who forsake your law.
[54] Your statutes have been my songs
in the house where I make my home.
[55] I remember your name in the night, O Yahweh,
and keep your law;
[56] this has been my practice,
that I have kept your precepts.

My hope is in you, O God, for your word is life. In the midst of scepticism and scorn I hold on to your promises, for I know they are faithful and true. I will sing of your mighty deeds with a joyful heart: in your house I wish to live for ever. I pray for those who have abandoned your ways, that you may find them and bring them home. Hear my prayer, O Lord.

16 OCTOBER

O Yahweh, I promise to keep your words

PSALM 119:57-64

[57] O Yahweh, you are my share;
I promise to keep your words.
[58] I seek your face with all my heart;
be true to your promise, take pity on me.
[59] I have considered your ways,
and turned my feet to your testimonies;
[60] I hurry without delay
to keep your commands.
[61] Though caught in the snares of the wicked,
I do not forget your law.
[62] I rise at midnight to praise you
because your ordinances are just.
[63] I befriend all those who fear you,
all who keep your precepts.
[64] Your faithful love fills the earth,
O Yahweh, teach me your judgements.

O Lord, you are everything to me. I have promised to try to follow your precepts, but in my weakness I rely upon your saving grace. When I am trapped by temptations, help me to be strong to fight and hold me by the hand. The whole earth is full of your love and your glory shines upon the whole of your creation. Night and day I praise you, O God. Amen.

17 OCTOBER

You are good, and you do good

PSALM 119:65-72

[65] Do good to your servant, O Yahweh,
according to your word.
[66] Teach me good judgement and knowledge,
for I trust in your commands.
[67] Before I was chastened I went astray,
but now I keep your word.
[68] You are good, and you do good;
teach me your statutes.
[69] The arrogant smear me with lies
but I keep your precepts with all my heart;
[70] their heart is swollen like fat
but I delight in your law.
[71] It is good that I had to suffer,
that I might learn your statutes.
[72] The law of your mouth means more to me
than thousands of pieces of gold and silver.

Your word is wonderful to me, Lord, and all that I do is done with your love in my heart. I have felt chastened when I have sinned, but you have always forgiven me and I have been able to return to my true home. Teach me your wisdom that I may teach it to others whom I meet on the pilgrimage of life. Protect me from the proud and arrogant who despise your word: may they come to know you, through your abundant grace. I worship you with a whole heart, O God. Amen.

18 OCTOBER

May your faithful love be there to console me

PSALM 119:73-80

[73] Your hands made me and formed me;
give me wisdom to learn your commands.
[74] Those who fear you rejoice when they see me,
because I have hoped in your word.
[75] O Yahweh, I know that your judgements are right;
even punishing me you keep faith with me.
[76] May your faithful love be there to console me,
as you have promised your servant.
[77] Give me your mercy that I may live,
for your law is my delight.
[78] May the arrogant be shamed for their lies against me,
but I will reflect on your precepts.
[79] Let those who fear you turn to me,
that they may know your judgements.
[80] May my heart be true to your statutes,
that I may not be put to shame.

Thank you, O Lord, for my creation and for your sustaining power within me. Your wisdom is far above human wisdom, and I know that your grace is enough for my needs. When you have allowed me to learn from the pain of my mistakes, I have been able to perceive your love; and your love is always nearby to comfort me. May your merciful care rest upon the faithful and may those without faith come to know you. Amen.

19 OCTOBER

In your faithful love, save my life

PSALM 119:81-88

[81] My soul faints as it longs for your freedom;
I put my hope in your word.
[82] My sight fails through seeking your promise;
I ask when you will comfort me,
[83] for I have become like a shrivelled wineskin,
but I do not forget your statutes.
[84] How long must your servant wait?
When will you punish those who persecute me?
[85] The arrogant dig traps for me
in defiance of your law.
[86] All your commands are sure;
O help me, they chase me with lies.
[87] They had almost swept me off the earth,
but I have not deserted your precepts.
[88] In your faithful love, save my life,
that I may obey the judgements you give.

Sometimes, O Lord, life seems very grim, for you appear to be far from me. I long to live in the freedom of your love once again, but I am trapped by the selfish ways of the world. Yet, deep down, I know that you are beside me, and that your love is sure and certain. I pray, therefore, that you will save from those enemies who attack me both from within and without. Hear my prayer, O God of grace. Amen.

20 OCTOBER

I am yours

PSALM 119:89-96

[89] O Yahweh, your word is eternal,
firmly fixed in the heavens;
[90] your faithfulness lasts from age to age,
as the earth which you formed stands firm;
[91] your judgements endure to this day,
for all that exists serves you.
[92] If your law had not been my delight,
I would have died in distress.
[93] I will never forget your precepts,
for you give me life through them.
[94] I am yours, O save me,
for I have sought your precepts.
[95] The wicked are waiting to kill me,
but I consider your judgements.
[96] I see limits to every perfection,
but your command is boundless.

Your word is fixed beyond the stars, O God, and your faithfulness is founded beyond this universe. The whole of creation is yours and all that exists belongs to you. Your love and your laws are my constant delight and I long to live in your glorious kingdom. Save me from falling and protect me from my enemies. I place my life in your care, O Lord, this day and always. Amen.

21 OCTOBER

Your commands make me wiser

PSALM 119:97-104

[97] O how I love your law;
I reflect on it all day long.
[98] Your commands make me wiser than my foes;
they stay with me forever;
[99] I am wiser than all my teachers,
your commands are with me forever;
[100] I understand more than the old,
because I keep your precepts.
[101] My foot avoids evil ways,
so that I may keep your word.
[102] I do not stray from your judgements,
for you yourself have taught me.
[103] How sweet are your words to my taste,
sweeter than honey to my mouth.
[104] From your precepts I gain understanding,
so I hate every path of untruth.

May your teaching give me wisdom, O Lord, and may your love grow within me. Help me to avoid wicked ways and hold me to the straight path of life. I do not wish to stray, but my human weakness is all too prevalent. The words of your revelation are wonderful to speak and I desire to live according to your word. Save me from falsehood and teach me your truth, O God. Amen.

22 OCTOBER

Your word is a lamp to my feet

PSALM 119:105-112

[105] Your word is a lamp to my feet,
your word is a light to my path.
[106] I have taken an oath and confirmed it,
to keep your righteous judgements.
[107] I am deeply distressed, O Yahweh,
revive me as you have promised.
[108] Accept, O Yahweh, my gifts of praise,
and instruct me in your judgements.
[109] I continually hold my life in my hand,
but I do not forget your law.
[110] The wicked have set a snare for me,
but I do not stray from your precepts.
[111] Your testimonies are my share forever;
they are, indeed, the joy of my heart.
[112] I set my heart on keeping your statutes,
to the very end.

The lamp of your word is ever before me, O God, and your light on my path is a sure guide. I have promised to serve you faithfully, and with your help I shall keep my word. When I stray, steer me back to righteous ways. When deceitful people try to entrap me in their falsehoods, keep my footsteps from straying. Your word is my joy, O Lord, and I worship you wholeheartedly. Amen.

23 OCTOBER

You are my refuge

PSALM 119:113-120

[113] I hate the two-faced people,
but I love your law.
[114] You are my refuge and shield;
I put my hope in your word.
[115] Leave me alone, you wicked;
I shall keep the commands of my God.
[116] Support me that I may live, as you said,
and do not let my hopes be dashed;
[117] support me, that I may be safe
and always be turned to your statutes.
[118] You reject all who stray from your statutes,
for all their deceit is in vain.
[119] You treat all earth's wicked as dross,
therefore I love your testimonies.
[120] I tremble before you in awe,
and I am afraid of your judgements.

Keep me from hypocrisy, Lord, and be my refuge and my shield. My entire hope is in your word and I love your precepts. Support and help me in difficult times that I may be safe from evil powers. I know that anything short of truth is unacceptable to you, so I ask for your guidance in keeping to your ways. I worship you in awe and wonder, O God. Amen.

24 OCTOBER

I am your servant

PSALM 119:121-128

[121] All my deeds have been just and right;
do not leave me to my foes.
[122] Guarantee your servant's welfare;
do not let the arrogant oppress me.
[123] My sight fails in seeking your safety
and the aims of your faithful promise;
[124] show your servant your faithful love,
and teach me your statutes;
[125] I am your servant, give me wisdom
to understand your judgements.
[126] It is time for Yahweh to act,
for they have broken your law.
[127] Because I love your commands
far above gold, fine gold,
[128] I rule my life by your precepts
and hate all deceptive paths.

I desire only to serve you, O Lord, and your faithful love grows deep within me. When arrogant people reject your word and persecute the faithful, may your justice be swift and sure. Grant me wisdom to understand the mysteries of your revelation, for I love your wonderful ways. Abide with me for the rest of my earthly life, O God, and guide me in the way that I should go. Amen.

25 OCTOBER

Your words bring light

PSALM 119:129-136

[129] Your judgements fill me with wonder,
therefore I observe them.
[130] Your words bring light as they are revealed,
which makes the simple understand.
[131] I pant with gaping mouth
in longing for your commands.
[132] Turn to me, have mercy on me,
as you turn to those who love your name.
[133] Keep my steps firm in your promise,
and let no sin gain hold over me.
[134] Free me from human oppression,
that I may keep your precepts.
[135] Let your face shine on your servant,
and teach me your statutes.
[136] My eyes stream with tears,
for your law is not obeyed.

Illuminate my mind with your word, O God, and give me the wisdom to follow your precepts. I long to do your will as far as I am able to, and I pray that you will grant me the grace to hold to my commitment. Free all peoples from cruel oppression and give your light to all nations. May your face shine upon them forever. Amen.

26 OCTOBER

Your justice is righteous forever

PSALM 119:137-144

[137] O Yahweh, you are just
and all your judgements are right;
[138] you gave all your judgements in justice
and in all faithfulness.
[139] My zeal is wearing me out,
for my foes ignore your words.
[140] Your promise is thoroughly proved,
and your servant loves it.
[141] Although I am small and despised,
I do not forget your precepts.
[142] Your justice is righteous forever,
and your law is true.
[143] Trouble and anguish have gripped me,
but your commands are my delight.
[144] Your judgements are right forever;
give me wisdom that I may live.

Your judgements are always righteous, O God, and you are ever faithful. I am trying to follow your ways, but life is sometimes difficult because some of those around me do not believe in you. When I am troubled, I pray that you will comfort me with your word. Grant me wisdom that I may live in your light forever. Hear my prayer, O Lord. Amen.

27 OCTOBER

You are near to me, O Yahweh

PSALM 119:145-152

[145] I call with all my heart;
hear me, O Yahweh, I will keep your statutes;
[146] I cry to you, O save me,
that I may obey your judgements;
[147] I rise before dawn and cry for help;
I put my hope in your words;
[148] my eyes stay open throughout the night,
that I may reflect on your words.
[149] Hear my voice in your faithful love;
in your justice, O Yahweh, preserve my life.
[150] The wicked conspire and draw near,
but they are far from your law.
[151] You are near to me, O Yahweh,
and all your commands are true.
[152] I have known for long from your judgements
that you have made them forever.

I cry to you for help, Lord, because evil powers are all around me. Each morning I call to you to guide me through the day, and it is a wonderful comfort to know that you are with me. By night I think about your word and my heart and mind are full of your faithful love. Your word is everlasting and your commandments are forever. I praise you, O God. Amen.

28 OCTOBER

See my distress and deliver me

Psalm 119:153-160

[153] See my distress and deliver me,
for I do not forget your law.
[154] Plead my cause and redeem me;
as you promised, give me new life.
[155] Salvation is far from the wicked,
for they do not seek your statutes.
[156] O Yahweh, your mercy is great;
renew my life according to your laws.
[157] My oppressors and foes are many,
but I do not swerve from your judgements.
[158] I look at the faithless with loathing;
they do not keep your commands.
[159] See how I keep your precepts, O Yahweh;
preserve my life by your faithful love.
[160] All your words are true,
and your righteous judgements endure forever.

Redeem me, O Lord, and renew my life. Have mercy on me and forgive my iniquities. When I am in distress, hear my prayer for help. The world is full of wickedness and there seems to be no end to the perfidy of faithless people. But in you I put my trust, for I know that your words are true and faithful. May I dwell with you in righteousness forever, O God. Amen.

29 OCTOBER

I wait for your freedom, O Yahweh

PSALM 119:161-168

[161] Rulers oppress me for nothing,
but my heart stands in awe of your words.
[162] I rejoice at your word
like one who finds great spoils.
[163] I hate and abhor what is false,
but I love your law.
[164] Seven times a day I praise you,
because of your righteous judgements.
[165] They have great peace who love your law,
nothing can make them trip.
[166] I wait for your freedom, O Yahweh,
and I keep your commands.
[167] My soul observes your judgements,
for I dearly love them.
[168] I keep your precepts and judgements,
for all my ways are before you.

All day I am filled with praise for you, O Lord, for your word is a great treasure for those who hear it and obey your commandments. Release your faithful people from oppression and grant your peace to those who love you. I rejoice in the freedom of your love and my soul is thirsty for your word. My whole life is open to you, O God, and I pray that you will form me into a citizen of your glorious kingdom. Amen.

30 OCTOBER

Come and seek your servant

PSALM 119:169-176

[169] May my cry come before you, O Yahweh,
give me wisdom by your word.
[170] May my prayer for favour reach you;
save me by your word.
[171] May my lips proclaim your praise,
because you teach me your statutes.
[172] May my tongue sing of your word,
for all your commands are just.
[173] May your hand be ready to help me,
for I have chosen your precepts.
[174] O Yahweh, I long for your freedom;
your law is my delight.
[175] Let me live that I may praise you,
and give me your judgements for help.
[176] I have strayed like a sheep that is lost;
come and seek your servant,
for I do not forget your commands.

Give me the wisdom that comes from reverence for your word, O God. May my prayers be acceptable in your eyes and may my lips proclaim your praise worthily. I long to sing of your love and of your mighty works. Grant me the freedom that your grace brings to those who devote their lives to you. Let me live daily in your kingdom and, if I stray, bring me back into your fold. Hear my prayer, O Lord. Amen.

31 OCTOBER

O Yahweh, save me from lying lips

Psalm 120

[1] I called to Yahweh in my trouble,
and he answered me.
[2] O Yahweh, save me from lying lips,
from deceitful tongues.
[3] What shall be done to you,
what is in store for you, deceitful tongue?
[4] Sharp arrows of the warrior,
and red-hot coals!
[5] My wretched lot is exile in Meshech,
to live by the tents of Kedar.
[6] I have lived too long
among those who hate peace.
[7] I am all for peace,
but when I speak, they call for war.

I give thanks for the many times you have answered my calls for help, Lord. Once again I am in need of your grace. I seem to be surrounded by falsehood and deceit. I pray that your truth will prevail and that those who do not know your ways may hear your call to righteousness. I long for your inward peace, O God, but I also pray that your peace will prevail throughout the earth. Amen.

1 NOVEMBER

My help comes from Yahweh

PSALM 121:1-4

[1] I lift up my eyes to the hills;
where will my help come from?
[2] My help comes from Yahweh,
who made heaven and earth.
[3] He will not allow your foot to slip;
your guardian will not slumber.
[4] The guardian of Israel
neither slumbers nor sleeps.

The hills seem eternal, O Lord, but they are fleeting creations compared with your eternity. I trust only in you for help, because you made the heavens and the earth; and all that exists is in the hollow of your hand. Watch over me by night and by day: stand beside me in times of peril. I praise you, O God, for you are my Saviour and my guardian. Amen.

2 NOVEMBER

Yahweh will keep you from all harm

PSALM 121:5-8

[5] Yahweh watches over you,
Yahweh, the shelter on your right;
[6] the sun will not harm you by day,
nor the moon by night.
[7] Yahweh will keep you from all harm,
he will guard your life;
[8] Yahweh will guard your coming and going,
both now and for eternity.

I know that nothing in heaven or on earth can harm me, Lord, when you are with me. Watch over all my doings and guide me in the right path. Keep me from harmful influences and preserve my life in safety. Wherever I go, I know that you will abide with me through any dangers that might beset me. I commend myself into your care, O God, from now until eternity. Amen.

3 NOVEMBER

Let us go to the house of Yahweh

PSALM 122:1-5

[1] I rejoiced when they said to me,
"Let us go to the house of Yahweh."
[2] Our feet are at your gates, O Jerusalem.
[3] Jerusalem is built as a city
that is firmly bound together;
[4] that is where the tribes ascend,
the tribes of Israel,
to praise the name of Yahweh,
as his law to Israel commands.
[5] The thrones of judgement are there,
the thrones of the house of David.

It is wonderful indeed, O God, to worship with the faithful community in your house. To enter the gates of heaven must be even more wonderful, and I long to be with you to eternity in your kingdom. Bring unity to the people you have chosen and may all the nations praise your name together. I stand before your throne and worship you with my whole heart and mind. Amen.

4 NOVEMBER

May peace be within you

PSALM 122:6-9

[6] Pray for the peace of Jerusalem:
"May those who love you prosper;
[7] may there be peace within your walls,
and safety within your citadels."
[8] For the sake of my brothers and friends,
I say, "May peace be within you."
[9] For the sake of the house of Yahweh our God,
I will seek your good.

May the peace of heaven spread throughout the world, O God, and may your faithful people live in safety always. Bring prosperity to all nations and grant that they may learn to share like brothers and sisters. Bring peace to my own heart and grant me a quiet mind as I face the problems of each day. May your goodness grow fruitfully in my innermost heart. Hear my prayer, O God. Amen.

5 NOVEMBER

O Yahweh, pity us

PSALM 123

[1] I lift my eyes to you
whose throne is in heaven.
[2] As the eyes of slaves
watch their master's hand,
or the eyes of a slave-girl

watch the hand of her mistress,
so we watch Yahweh our God
until he shows us his mercy.
[3] O Yahweh, pity us, have pity,
for we have suffered scorn enough,
[4] much scorn from the proud
and contempt from the arrogant.

I worship before the majesty of your heavenly throne, O God, and I praise you with my whole heart. May I be your servant always, for you are like a loving father. Have mercy on me when I do wrong and grant me a safe passage through the storms of life. May those who scorn the faithful come to know your glory also, O Lord. Amen.

6 NOVEMBER

If Yahweh had not been for us

PSALM 124

[1] If Yahweh had not been for us,
(let Israel say it again!)
[2] if Yahweh had not been for us,
when we were attacked,
[3] when anger flared up against us,
we would have been swallowed whole.
[4] The flood would have drowned us;
the torrent would have swept above us;
[5] raging rapids would have swept us away.
[6] Praise be to Yahweh,
who would not let us be torn apart.
[7] We escaped like a bird

from the fowler's net;
the net has been broken
and we have escaped.
[8] Our help is in the name of Yahweh,
who made heaven and earth.

Thank you, Lord, for the many times when you have saved me from harm. If you are with me, I know that ultimately nothing can hurt me, despite the dangers and temptations of each day. I give you praise for releasing me from the bonds of sin which were holding me fast. In your name, O Lord, I rejoice as I travel towards the gates of your kingdom. I praise you mightily. Amen.

7 NOVEMBER

Yahweh encircles his people

Psalm 125:1-2

[1] If you trust in Yahweh you are like Mount Zion:
it cannot be shaken,
it stands firm for ever.
[2] As the mountains encircle Jerusalem,
so Yahweh encircles his people,
both now and forever.

When I trust in you, O God, I feel as safe as if I were in your heavenly city. Nothing will harm me when you are with me. I will stand firm in the faith until the day you call me homewards. Your power encircles the faithful with impregnable mountain defences. Keep me safe forever, Lord. Amen.

8 NOVEMBER

Do good, O Yahweh, to those who are good

PSALM 125:3-5

[3] The rule of the wicked must not continue
over the heritage of the upright,
or the upright might turn their own hands
to evil.
[4] Do good, O Yahweh, to those who are good,
the honest of heart.
[5] But those who turn to wicked ways
are banished by Yahweh with evil-doers.
May Israel have peace!

May wicked powers collapse under the eye of your justice, Lord, and may those who pursue virtue prevail. Keep the faithful within your kingdom and guard them from temptation. May the honest of heart know your blessing and may they be strengthened in following good paths. Bring peace from evil powers to your faithful people. Hear my prayer this day, O God. Amen.

9 NOVEMBER

Yahweh did great things for us

PSALM 126:1-3

[1] When Yahweh returned the exiles to Zion
we were like dreamers,
[2] with mouths full of laughter,
tongues singing with joy.

Word passed round the nations,
"These are Yahweh's great deeds for them!"
[3] Yes! Yahweh did great things for us,
and we are glad.

When you returned me from the exile of sin to the joys of your kingdom, Lord, life was wonderful and my heart was full of praiseful song. May all peoples know this joy and may all nations become part of your kingdom. You have done great things for me and I am filled with delight at the marvel of your constant love. Amen.

10 NOVEMBER

The sower returns singing joyfully

PSALM 126:4-6

[4] O Yahweh, restore our fortunes
like torrents in the south.
[5] To sow in tears means joyful reaping.
[6] The sower who weeps
as he carries the seed,
returns singing joyfully,
bearing the sheaves.

Let your living waters flow through my arid soul, O God. I have shed the tears of repentance and I long to know again the harvest of your forgiving love. I have been in a trough of despair, but you have lifted my head. I see before me the harvest fields and the rich sheaves waiting to be carried home. I thank you and praise you, O God. Amen

11 NOVEMBER

Unless Yahweh builds the house

PSALM 127:1-2

[1] Unless Yahweh builds the house,
its builders work in vain.
Unless Yahweh guards the city,
the watchmen guard in vain.
[2] It is vain to rise early
and stay up late,
toiling for food;
he provides for his loved ones while they sleep.

I pray, O God, that you will form my character and that you will guide me in all my actions. I know that if you are within me I shall stand in the day of trial. Give me my daily bread and watch over my concerns while I sleep. I trust in you alone, O God, and I know that if you are not beside me then my living is in vain. Hear my prayer, and let my cry come unto you. Amen.

12 NOVEMBER

Children are Yahweh's reward

PSALM 127:3-5

[3] Yahweh gives sons as a gift,
children are his reward.
[4] Like arrows in a bowman's hand
are the sons you father when young.
[5] Blessed are those with quivers full of them;
they will not be dismayed,
fighting foes at the gate.

Bless my family and others whom I love, O Lord. Give those who have no children of their own a very special blessing and grant them a double portion of your love. To those who have children, grant the wisdom to nurture their offspring with love, that all of them may grow with your kingdom in their hearts. Defend those who love you Lord, and watch over their homes. Amen.

13 NOVEMBER

Blessed are all who walk in his ways

PSALM 128:1-4

[1] Blessed are all who fear Yahweh,
who walk in his ways.
[2] You will eat the fruits of your work;
you will be happy and prosperous.
[3] Your wife will be like a fruitful vine
within your house.
Your children round your table
will be like olive shoots.
[4] Those are the kind of blessings
that fall on those who fear Yahweh.

May those who love you and reverence your name receive your guidance throughout their lives, O God. May they be richly blessed and may their days upon earth be happy, as they prepare for the rich new life of heaven. Give to your servant also a share in your blessing, that I may overcome all dangers and temptations in this life, and at the end enter your kingdom full of holiness and joy. Amen.

14 NOVEMBER

May you live to see your children's children

PSALM 128:5-6

[5] May Yahweh bless you from Zion
all the days you live;
may you see Jerusalem prosper,
and live to see your children's children.
[6] Peace be on Israel!

May your peace always fill my heart, Lord, and may your blessing go with me all the days of my life. May the faithful prosper in your kingdom and may they grow in love and grace. Grant all your children wisdom to do what is right, that they may at the end enter the gates of your heavenly city and partake of your joyful feast. Hear my prayer, O God. Amen.

15 NOVEMBER

Yahweh is victorious

PSALM 129:1-4

[1] Since I was young they have often attacked me.
Let Israel say it again:
[2] since I was young they have often attacked me,
but they have never vanquished me.
[3] Like ploughmen they cut my back,
cutting their furrows long,
[4] but Yahweh is victorious,
and cuts me free from their wicked ropes.

Protect me from the wiles of Satan Lord, for temptations have beset me throughout my life. Yet, with your strength within me I have survived in the faith, and it is my prayer that I should continue in the same until my life's end. My firm hope is that you will give me the victory and that you will free me from the bondage of my sins. Grant me your salvation, O Lord. Amen.

16 NOVEMBER

We bless you in the name of Yahweh

PSALM 129:5-8

[5] May all who hate Zion
be repulsed in confusion;
[6] may they be like grass clinging to roofs
which withers before it can grow,
[7] never to fill the reaper's hands,
nor give the harvester an armful;
[8] may those who pass by never say,
"The blessing of Yahweh be with you;
we bless you in the name of Yahweh."

May those who despise the city of God and all it stands for, come to see the error of their ways, O God. They will never truly prosper while they are ignorant of your love and faithfulness. But if they can be brought to an understanding of your ways, perhaps they will repent and try to pursue righteousness. Hear my prayer, gracious Lord. Amen.

17 NOVEMBER

O Yahweh, I call to you out of the depths

PSALM 130:1-4

[1] O Yahweh, I call to you out of the depths;
[2] O Yahweh, hear my cry;
Let your ears give attention to my cry for mercy.
[3] O Yahweh, if you recorded sins,
O Yahweh, who could stand?
[4] But you are forgiving,
and so you are revered.

When I am in the depths of despair, O God, hear my cry for help. I trust in your great mercy, for although my sins are many, I know that your love is eternal. No one can stand without your aid; and if you remember all my shortcomings I am lost. But you have promised forgiveness for those who repent, so I turn to you in hope. Hear my prayer, O Lord. Amen.

18 NOVEMBER

Put your hope in Yahweh

PSALM 130:5-8

[5] I wait for Yahweh, my soul waits,
I put my hope in his word.
[6] My soul waits for Yahweh
more than watchmen wait for the dawn.
[7] Israel, put your hope in Yahweh,
for with Yahweh there is faithful love,
and full redemption.

[8] He will redeem Israel
from all their sins.

How I wait for you to come, Lord! My heart longs for your appearing. I trust in your word, for you have promised redemption for all your faithful people. Like a watchman on the walls of a besieged city, I watch for you. As soon as you come to me, I know that the forces of evil will disperse. Hear my prayer, O God. Amen.

19 NOVEMBER

My soul is like a weaned child

PSALM 131

[1] O Yahweh, my heart is not proud,
my eyes are not raised too high;
I do not take part in great affairs,
in marvels beyond my capacity;
[2] I keep myself in calm and quietness,
like a weaned child with its mother,
my soul within me is like a weaned child.
[3] Israel, hope in Yahweh,
now and for eternity.

O God, my pride is gone, for I know that before you I am so small and insignificant. What are the affairs of this world compared with your love? What are human creations compared with your creation of heaven and earth? I pray for your peace, for the inner stillness that comes from being close to you each day. You are the hope of my life, O God, and my final hope is for eternal life with you. Amen.

20 NOVEMBER

Rise up, Yahweh

PSALM 132:1-10

[1] O Yahweh, remember David,
and all the trouble he endured.
[2] He swore an oath to Yahweh,
a vow to the Mighty One of Jacob,
[3] "I will not enter my house,
nor go to my bed;
[4] I will not allow myself to sleep,
nor even close my eyes,
[5] until I find a place for Yahweh,
a house for the Mighty One of Jacob."
[6] We heard it said in Ephrathah,
and again in the fields of Jaar,
[7] "Let us go to his dwelling-place
and worship at his footstool."
[8] Rise up, Yahweh, and come to your home,
you and the ark of your might.
[9] Clothe your priests in righteousness;
may your faithful sing for joy.
[10] For the sake of your servant David,
do not reject your anointed.

I have promised to serve you all my life, O Lord, and I pray for your strength and grace to persevere in this service. I long for your presence and I search constantly for signs that you are with me. I love to go to your holy places to worship with the faithful community. I pray that you will reveal yourself as I worship and adore your holy name. Abide with me, O God. Amen.

21 NOVEMBER

An oath Yahweh will not break

Psalm 132:11-12

[11] Yahweh swore this oath to David,
an oath he will not break,
"I will choose your successor
from among your own sons;
[12] if your sons keep my covenant
and the statutes which I teach them,
then they will sit on your throne
for evermore."

I pray that I may have the grace to keep your covenant, O God, and I pray for the coming generations, that they may hear your voice and obey it. I know that you will walk with those who are sincere in their love for you, and I know that your holy word is unbreakable. I therefore pray that you will abide with the whole community of your faithful people until your purposes on earth are completed. Hear my prayer, O Lord. Amen.

22 NOVEMBER

Yahweh has chosen Zion for his home

Psalm 132:13-18

[13] For Yahweh has chosen Zion;
he wants it for his home,
[14] "This is where I will rest forever;
I will sit enthroned here,
as I have wished;

[15] I will bless her with bountiful produce,
and fill her needy with food;
[16] I will clothe her priests with salvation,
and her faithful will shout with joy.
[17] I will raise there a line
of descendants for David,
and light a lamp for my anointed.
[18] I will clothe his foes in shame,
and crown him with splendour."

I thank you, Lord, for the ideal of Zion as your dwelling place, and I pray that I may be a citizen of your kingdom. Bless all those who dwell in the kingdom of heaven upon earth and grant them their daily needs. For all who serve you in the community of the faithful I ask your aid, that they may be filled with the joy of your saving grace. For all your anointed servants, O God, I pray victory over temptation and evil. Amen.

23 NOVEMBER

How good it is to live together

PSALM 133

[1] How good and delightful it is
to live together
as brothers in unity!
[2] It is like precious oil
poured on the head, running over the beard,
running down Aaron's beard
and onto his robes.
[3] It is like dew of Hermon
falling on Mount Zion;

for Yahweh gives his blessing there,
life for evermore.

I thank you, O Lord, for the joy of belonging to the family of the faithful. I pray that all those who know you may come together as one body, so that their prayer and praise may sound in unison throughout the world. For all those with responsibilities among the faithful, I pray your guidance and help. Grant a rich blessing, O God, to those who lead their lives in your glorious light. Amen.

24 NOVEMBER

May Yahweh bless you

PSALM 134

[1] Praise Yahweh,
all you servants of Yahweh,
who serve at night
in Yahweh's house.
[2] Raise your hands
in the sanctuary,
and praise Yahweh.
[3] May Yahweh,
maker of heaven and earth,
bless you from Zion.

I will praise your name forever, O Lord, and I offer my whole life to you as I journey towards your sanctuary in heaven. I worship you with my whole heart: may my every thought, deed and word be a prayer in your name. By night I will watch in prayer and by day I will walk in faith. I glorify you for the beauties of your creation, O God, and may all creatures upon earth receive your blessing. Amen.

25 NOVEMBER

Praise Yahweh, for Yahweh is good

PSALM 135:1-4

[1] Praise Yahweh!
Praise the name of Yahweh,
praise him, you servants of Yahweh,
[2] you who serve in the house of Yahweh,
in the courts of the house of our God.
[3] Praise Yahweh, for Yahweh is good;
sing to his name, his gracious name.
[4] For Yahweh chose Jacob to be his own,
and Israel to be his prized possession.

I praise you, O Lord, and with all your servants I worship you with thanksgiving for the many blessings you have given to those who have faith in your providential care. I love to sing your praises in the gathering of the faithful and I glorify your holy name with all my heart and soul. I know you have chosen each one of us, O God, and it is wonderful to be your child. Amen.

26 NOVEMBER

Yahweh does whatever he wills

Psalm 135:5-7

[5] I know that Yahweh is great,
that Yahweh is greater than all the gods.
[6] Yahweh does whatever he wills,
in the heavens and on the earth,
in the seas to the furthest depths.
[7] He forms clouds from the ends of the earth;
the lightning splits them and it rains;
he brings the winds from his stores.

Your name is great, O God, and the whole earth resounds with your praise. Your active will is evident throughout the whole of your creation. I pray that I may grow closer to you, and that I may strive in my little way to do your will. Your creation is a marvel to my eyes and your power – as written in the wind and the rain, in the lightning and the storm – is wonderful in my sight. I praise you, O Lord. Amen.

27 NOVEMBER

O Yahweh, your name will last forever

Psalm 135:8-14

[8] He killed the first-born of Egypt,
the first-born both of people and beasts;
[9] he sent signs and portents into Egypt,
against Pharaoh and all his subjects.
[10] He subdued many nations
and killed mighty kings,

[11] Sihon, king of the Amorites,
Og, king of Bashan
and all the kings of Canaan,
[12] and he gave their land as a heritage,
a heritage to his people Israel.
[13] O Yahweh, your name will last forever,
your fame, O Yahweh, throughout the ages,
[14] for Yahweh vindicates his people
and has compassion on his servants.

I thank you, O God, for leading your people in past times, and I pray that you will continue to act on behalf of the faithful community now and in the future. Your deeds are wonderful, and the signs of your presence in the world are clearly visible to the eye of faith. Your name is eternal and your vindicated people will praise you always. I praise you, O Lord, for your great compassion and love. Amen.

28 NOVEMBER

Bless Yahweh!

PSALM 135:15-21

[15] The nations' idols are silver and gold,
made by human hands;
[16] they have mouths and cannot speak;
[17] they have ears and cannot hear;
they have mouths and cannot breathe.
[18] Those who make them are just like them,
and so are all who trust in them.
[19] Bless Yahweh, house of Israel!
Bless Yahweh, house of Aaron!

[20] Bless Yahweh, house of Levi!
Bless Yahweh, all who fear him!
[21] Blessed be Yahweh from Zion,
he who lives in Jerusalem.
Praise Yahweh!

O God, deliver the nations of the world from false beliefs and values. May the powers of evil be defeated and may the whole world resound with your praise alone. Your faithful people give thanks and bless your holy name. The chosen respond with love and reverence to your blessing. Your followers praise you in their sanctuaries, Lord, and your name is blessed constantly. I glorify you forever. Amen.

29 NOVEMBER

His faithful love endures forever

PSALM 136:1-9

[1] Give thanks to Yahweh, for he is good;
for his faithful love endures forever.
[2] Give thanks to the God of gods;
for his faithful love endures forever.
[3] Give thanks to the Lord of lords;
for his faithful love endures forever.
[4] To him who alone does great marvels;
for his faithful love endures forever.
[5] Who by his wisdom made the heavens;
for his faithful love endures forever.
[6] Who spread the world out on the waters;
for his faithful love endures forever.
[7] Who made the mighty lights;

for his faithful love endures forever.
[8] The sun to rule the day;
for his faithful love endures forever.
[9] the moon and stars to rule the night;
for his faithful love endures forever.

I give thanks to you, O God, for your great goodness and mercy. I glorify you for your creative power in the universe. The continents and the oceans are full of your wonders: the sun, the moon and the galaxies are signs of your presence. Your faithful love is eternal, O Lord, and I pray that I may know your touch, that I may reflect your love within my soul. I praise you mightily. Amen.

30 NOVEMBER

Give thanks to the God of heaven

Psalm 136:10-26

[10] Who killed the first-born of Egypt;
for his faithful love endures forever.
[11] And brought Israel out from among them;
for his faithful love endures forever.
[12] With a strong hand and outstretched arm;
for his faithful love endures forever.
[13] Who split the Red Sea apart;
for his faithful love endures forever.
[14] And brought Israel through its midst;
for his faithful love endures forever.
[15] But drowned Pharaoh and all his army;
for his faithful love endures forever.
[16] Who led his people through the desert;
for his faithful love endures forever.

[17] Who killed mighty kings;
for his faithful love endures forever.
[18] Who slaughtered famous kings;
for his faithful love endures forever.
[19] Sihon, king of the Amorites;
for his faithful love endures forever.
[20] Og, king of Bashan;
for his faithful love endures forever.
[21] And gave their land as a heritage;
for his faithful love endures forever.
[22] A heritage to his servant Israel;
for his faithful love endures forever.
[23] He remembered us when we were down;
for his faithful love endures forever.
[24] And freed us from our enemies;
for his faithful love endures forever.
[25] He gives food to all creatures;
for his faithful love endures forever.
[26] Give thanks to the God of heaven;
for his faithful love endures forever.

For your mighty acts in the history of the human race, I thank you, O Lord. I praise you for the heritage of the faith that has come down to me through past generations. I pray that you will free me from all hostile powers and that you will lead me to the promised land of your kingdom. I thank you for your daily providential care and for your faithful and eternal love. I praise you wholeheartedly. Amen.

1 DECEMBER

How could we sing in a foreign land?

PSALM 137:1-6

[1] By the rivers of Babylon we sat and wept
when we remembered Zion.
[2] There on the willows
we hung our harps,
[3] for our captors asked us to sing them songs,
our captors demanded songs of joy:
"Sing us one of the songs of Zion."
[4] How could we sing the songs of Yahweh
in a foreign land?
[5] If I forget you, Jerusalem,
may my right hand forget its skill;
[6] may my tongue cling to the roof of my mouth
if I do not remember you.

In past times, O God, I have wept because I have been far from you. I have been a captive of my own selfishness, and the evil powers of the world have held me in thrall. The scorn of the faithless has been painful. But nevertheless, you have brought me back to yourself, and I have come again to the gates of your kingdom. I will praise you forever, Lord. The riches of your grace are in my mind always. Amen.

2 DECEMBER

O Yahweh, remember when Jerusalem fell

Psalm 137:7-9

[7] O Yahweh, remember the deeds of the Edomites,
on the day when Jerusalem fell.
They cried, "Tear it down! Tear it down!
Tear it down to its very foundations!"
[8] Daughter of Babylon, doomed to destruction,
blessed be he who repays you
for what you have done to us,
[9] he who seizes your children
and dashes them against the rocks.

I pray for the destruction of the evil powers of Satan, Lord, and for the growth of the ideal Jerusalem in the hearts of all peoples. For those who treat with cruelty the poor and needy, I ask your certain and unswerving judgement. For those who scorn your faithful people, I pray an end to their wicked ways. May a knowledge of your love grow throughout the world, O God. Hear my prayer, I beseech you. Amen.

3 DECEMBER

May they sing of the ways of Yahweh

Psalm 138:1-6

[1] O Yahweh, I thank you with all my heart,
I will sing your praise before the gods.
[2] I will bow before your holy Temple
to praise your name for your faithful love
and your constancy.

You have made your word as wide as the heavens.
[3] When I called to you, you answered me
and gave new strength to my heart.
[4] May all earth's kings praise you, O Yahweh,
when they hear the words of your mouth.
[5] May they sing of the ways of Yahweh,
for the glory of Yahweh is great.
[6] Sublime as he is, Yahweh looks on the lowly,
but the proud he regards from afar.

I thank you and praise you, O Lord, for your faithful and constant love. I will worship you in your sanctuary and glorify your name forever. You have answered my prayers and given me strength, and I pray that I may abide with you always. May the rulers of the world come to know you and may they praise you mightily. Thank you, O God, for revealing yourself to the meek and lowly of heart. Amen.

4 DECEMBER

You stretch out your hand

PSALM 138:7-8

[7] Though I walk surrounded by trouble,
you guard my life;
you stretch out your hand
against my foes' anger.
[8] Yahweh will achieve his purpose for me.
O Yahweh, your faithful love lasts forever,
do not leave your work unfinished.

When I am walking in darkness, Lord, shine the light of your love upon me. Watch over me and guard my pathways. Help me to defeat those enemies who attack me both from within and from without. May your plans for me come to fruition and may I be faithful to my calling. Your faithful love is eternal and I know that the whole universe is in your providential care. I praise you, O God. Amen.

5 DECEMBER

O Yahweh, you know all

PSALM 139:1-6

[1] You examined me, O Yahweh, and you know me.
[2] You know when I sit and when I rise;
you know my thoughts from far off,
[3] you watch when I walk or lie down,
you know all the paths that I take.
[4] Before I have spoken a word,
O Yahweh, you know all about it.
[5] You keep close guard, behind and before me;
you spread your hand over me.
[6] Knowledge so great is beyond my grasp,
too high for me to attain.

When I meditate upon your ways, Lord, I realise that my every thought is known to you and that my life is written in your book of judgement. I pray that you will watch over my growth in your kingdom and that your hand will pluck me from the evil one when he comes to tempt me. Your wisdom is beyond my understanding, but I long to know more of your love. I praise you, O God. Amen.

6 DECEMBER

Where could I go from your spirit?

PSALM 139:7-12

[7] Where could I go from your spirit?
Where could I flee from your face?
[8] If I climb up to heaven, you are there;
if I make my bed in the grave
you are there.
[9] If I fly on the wings of the dawn
or dwell beyond the seas,
[10] even there your hand will guide me,
your right hand will hold me fast.
[11] If I say that the darkness will hide me
and the light become night for me,
[12] even darkness is not dark to you
the night will be bright as the day,
for the dark is like light to you.

Your Spirit is in every wind that blows through the universe, Lord, and your presence is manifest to me in the whisper of the dawn upon the darkness. Your light floods through the whole of heaven and earth and even within the spaciousness of death your lamp is shining before me. Guide me and hold me fast as I journey onwards, O God, and lead me to the gleaming steps that will take me to the gates of heaven. Amen.

7 DECEMBER

I praise you because I am wonderfully made

PSALM 139:13-16

[13] For you made my innermost self;
you formed me in my mother's womb.
[14] I praise you because I am wonderfully made.
All that you do is wonderful;
that I know very well.
[15] Nothing about me was secret from you
when I was made in the secret place,
when I was formed in the depths of the earth.
[16] Your eyes could see my embryo.
All my days were inscribed in your book
before any one of them came to be.

I thank you, Lord, because you have made my soul and body so wonderfully. My inmost self is your creation and all my thoughts have grown from the fountain of your love. You have watched over me from the womb until now, and I pray that you will watch over me until the day I die. I have no secrets from you, and so you know my weaknesses, but you also know my longing to love and worship you. I praise you, O God. Amen.

8 DECEMBER

O God, examine me and test me

PSALM 139:17-24

[17] How mysterious, O God, are your thoughts to me;
how many they are!

[18] More than grains of sand,
they cannot be counted;
when I lose count, I am still with you.
[19] If only, O God, you would kill the wicked.
Violent people, keep far from me!
[20] They speak about you blasphemously,
your enemies dismiss your thoughts.
[21] O Yahweh, I hate those who hate you,
and loathe those who rise up against you.
[22] I hate them with undying hatred,
and count them as my foes.
[23] O God, examine me and know my heart,
test me, and know my anxious thoughts.
[24] See that my way does not lead to my ruin,
and guide me on the eternal road.

I meditate upon your mysteries, O Lord, and I am lost in wonder at your holiness and majesty. You have created so many marvels that they cannot be counted, and each one is a thought from you. Yet, there are people who reject your love, and they are far from you. I pray that I shall always be near to you and that you will measure my needs, as you have done in past times. Guide me each day, O God. Amen.

9 DECEMBER

Save me, O Yahweh, from evil-doers

PSALM 140:1-6

[1] Save me, O Yahweh, from evil-doers;
keep me out of the way of the violent,
[2] whose hearts are bent on evil schemes,

who spend their days provoking wars.
[3] Their tongues are sharp as serpents' fangs;
vipers' venom is under their lips.
[4] Keep me, O Yahweh, from wicked hands;
protect me from the violent mob
who try to thrust me out of the way.
[5] The proud set hidden traps for me,
they wait for me with nets and snares.
[6] I said, "O Yahweh, you are my God."
Listen, O Yahweh, to my prayers.

Protect me from evil, O Lord, and help me to withstand the wiles of Satan. When people weave wicked plots and start conflicts, I pray that you will foil their designs. Keep me far from deceit and violence and guide me through the maze of pathways which lie before me. If you will walk with me, O God, I know that I will be safe from all harm. Hear my prayer, I beseech you. Amen.

10 DECEMBER

The upright will live in your sight

PSALM 140:7-13

[7] O Yahweh, God, my saving strength,
you shield my head when battle comes.
[8] O Yahweh, do not grant them
their wishes against me;
do not let the wicked
gain by their evil.
[9] May the heads of those who hem me in
be covered with trouble their own lips
have caused.

[10] May red-hot coals rain down on them;
let them sink in pits and never rise.
[11] May slanderers find no place to rest;
may repeated thrusts bring down the violent.
[12] I know that Yahweh secures justice to the poor
and makes common cause with the needy.
[13] Surely the righteous will praise your name;
the upright will live in your sight.

Watch over the poor and needy, Lord, and protect them from those who seek illicit gain. May your justice prevail where corruption is rife, and may your enemies fail to achieve their wicked aims. All those who value righteousness will praise you and they will strive to follow your ways. You are my shield and strength, O God. Abide with me, I pray you. Amen.

11 DECEMBER

Let not my heart be inclined to do evil

PSALM 141:1-7

[1] O Yahweh, I call to you, come to me quickly,
hear my voice when I call to you.
[2] May my prayer be like incense rising before you,
my uplifted hands like the evening sacrifice.
[3] O Yahweh, mount a guard on my mouth;
keep watch on the door of my lips.
[4] Let not my heart be inclined to do evil,
to join in the deeds of the wicked.
I shall not share in their delights!
[5] I would rather be struck by the just;
such is kindness.

Let him rebuke me, it is like an anointing,
my head makes it welcome.
My prayer is always against the deeds of evil-doers;
[6] their rulers will end being cast from the rocks,
then the wicked will know
that my words were well spoken.
[7] They will say,
"Like the ploughman who breaks up the earth,
our bones are all strewn
at the mouth of the grave."

Help me to control my thoughts and my actions, O Lord, and may my mouth speak only what is good. Remove me from the company of the wicked, for they are creating their own destruction. If I deserve rebuke, I will accept it gladly; but my prayer is for peace from the forces of evil. I pray to you constantly, O God, and my hope is in your saving grace. Amen.

12 DECEMBER

Do not leave me to die

PSALM 141:8-10

[8] But my eyes are turned towards you, O Lord
Yahweh;
you are my refuge, do not leave me to die.
[9] Save me from snares,
from the traps of the wicked.
[10] Let the wicked all fall
into their own nets, while I pass by safely.

I look only to you for help, O Lord, for you alone are my refuge. Save me from the snares of temptation and from the traps of the deceitful. May the wicked be caught in nets of their own devising. I pray that you will carry me through each day safely, despite the dangers that surround me. If you are walking beside me, O God, I will fear nothing, not even death, for I know that you will always be my defence. Amen.

13 DECEMBER

I cry out aloud to Yahweh

PSALM 142:1-4

[1] I cry out aloud to Yahweh,
I cry aloud to Yahweh for mercy.
[2] I pour out my worries before him,
I declare my troubles to his face.
[3] When my spirit is faint within me,
you are there to guide my steps.
In the path where I walk
they have hidden a trap for me.
[4] Look to my right hand and see!
There is no friend concerned for me.
I have no way of escape,
and no one cares for my life.

Have mercy on me, O Lord, when I am in distress. I will share all my troubles with you and I will confess all that is in my heart. When my spirit is burning low, strengthen me: when I am faint, support me. There are many traps in my path and I have no friend but you to be concerned for me. No one cares if I live or die, but only you, O God. In you I put my trust, for you are the fountain of life. Amen.

14 DECEMBER

The righteous will gather around me

PSALM 142:5-7

[5] O Yahweh, I cry to you,
saying, "You are my refuge,
my share of the land of the living."
[6] O Yahweh, listen to my cry,
for I am brought very low.
Save from those who trouble me,
from those who are too strong for me.
[7] Set me free from prison,
so that I may praise your name.
Then the righteous will gather around me,
because you give me my due reward.

I call to you for help, O God, for you are the one who sustains me throughout my life. When I am in low spirits, I cry to you: save me from those who persecute me. My enemies are strong and I am weak. Set me free from this prison of despair, that I may praise your name among the faithful. My reward is to love you forever, Lord. Amen.

15 DECEMBER

No one alive is guiltless to you

PSALM 143:1-6

[1] O Yahweh, hear my prayer;
listen to my supplications,
by your constancy and justice;
answer me.

[2] Do not bring your servant to trial,
for no one alive is guiltless to you.
[3] The enemy pursues me,
crushing my life to the ground,
forcing me into the darkness
like those long dead.
[4] My spirit faints within me;
my very heart is dismayed.
[5] My thoughts return to times long past;
reflecting on all your works,
and I think about all that you did.
[6] I stretch out my hands to you;
I thirst for you like an arid land.

My spirit thirsts for your presence, O Lord: do not leave me alone in this arid desert of hopelessness. I pray to you constantly, for I believe your love and justice are infinite. When the enemies of good surround me, I rely upon your strong arm to guide me through the darkness of despair. I long to be happy again, O God, to sing your praises as before, when your blessings were so apparent to me. Hear my prayer, I beseech you. Amen.

16 DECEMBER

Show me the way I must go

PSALM 143:7-12

[7] O Yahweh, answer me quickly;
my spirit faints with worry.
Do not turn your face from me,
or I will be like those cast into the pit.
[8] At dawn bring me word of your faithful love,
for I have put my trust in you;

show me the way I must go,
for I lift up my soul to you.
[9] O Yahweh, save me from my foes,
for I find protection in you.
[10] Teach me to do your will,
for you are my God;
may your gracious spirit guide me
on to level ground.
[11] For the sake of your name
save my life, O Yahweh;
in your righteousness,
save me from trouble.
[12] By your faithful love,
silence my foes;
kill all my enemies,
for I am your servant.

Each morning I wait for you, O Lord, for a day without you beside me would be empty indeed. Help me each day to face up to the problems and dangers that surround me. Teach me the way that I should go and reveal to me your will, that I may strive to achieve it. May your Holy Spirit abide with me and may your faithful love fill my heart, that I may influence those around me. Hear my prayer, O God. Amen.

17 DECEMBER

Blessed be Yahweh, my rock

Psalm 144:1-2

[1] Blessed be Yahweh, my rock,
who trains my hands for war,
my fingers for the fight.

[2] He is my faithful love, my fortress,
my stronghold and my Saviour,
my shield, my place of refuge,
who subdues nations under me.

May your holy name be blessed forever, Lord, for you are the Rock of my life and my fortress in times of danger. Teach me the way to fight the powers of wickedness which beset me, and fill my soul with your constant love, that I may abide in the evil day. You are my shield, and with you beside me I can subdue those enemies who attack me both from within and without. I praise you, O God. Amen.

18 DECEMBER

Frail mortals are like a breath

PSALM 144:3-8

[3] O Yahweh, what are humans,
that you should show them care?
What are frail mortals,
that you spare them a thought?
[4] They are like a breath,
their days but fleeting shadows.
[5] O Yahweh, split heaven and descend,
touch the mountains to make them smoke.
[6] Send down lightning to shatter the foe,
shoot your arrows and scatter them.
[7] Stretch down your hand from above,
deliver me and rescue me
from mighty seas and aliens' hands
[8] whose words are worthless,
whose oaths are false.

My life is but a breath compared with your eternity, O Lord, and I am but a fleeting shadow in the face of your infinite and never failing light. Show yourself yet again to the enemies of righteousness, that they may scatter before your glorious revelation. Rescue me from false and evil powers, O God, and take my hand in yours. Hear my prayer this day. Amen.

19 DECEMBER

Blessed are those whose God is Yahweh

PSALM 144:9-15

[9] I will sing you a new song, O God,
songs to the sound of a ten-stringed lyre,
[10] to the One who gives victory to kings,
and saves David your servant from the deadly sword.
[11] Deliver and save me from aliens' hands,
whose words are worthless,
whose oaths are false.
[12] Our sons in their youth will be thriving plants,
our daughters like pillars
adorning a palace.
[13] Our barns will be filled with all kinds of food,
our sheep grow by thousands,
by many tens of thousands,
[14] and fat cattle in our fields.
No more breaching of walls or captives in exile,
no screams of anguish in our streets.
[15] Blessed are those of whom this is true.
Blessed are those whose God is Yahweh.

I will sing your praises yet again, O God, for you are the one who gives the victory to your faithful people. Deliver me from my enemies and give me your abundant blessing in this life and the next. May all your enemies be subdued and may the righteous be brought into your kingdom. May the nations praise you for your gracious and bountiful love. Amen.

20 DECEMBER

I will bless your name forever and ever

PSALM 145:1-7

[1] I will exalt you, O God my king,
and bless your name forever and ever.
[2] Every day I will bless you,
and praise your name forever and ever.
[3] Yahweh is great and most worthy of praise;
his greatness is far beyond measure.
[4] Each age will praise your deeds to another
and tell of your mighty deeds.
[5] They will speak of your glorious
splendour of majesty,
and I will ponder your wonderful works.
[6] They will tell of your awesome power,
and I will recount your greatness.
[7] They will rejoice in your great generosity,
and joyfully sing of your righteousness.

You are my King and my God and I will praise you while I have breath. Past ages have told of your mighty deeds and I thank you that you have revealed your wonderful love to humankind. Your splendour is unimaginable: your glory is beyond description. Show yourself to this generation, O God, that all peoples may honour and adore your exalted name. Amen.

21 DECEMBER

Yahweh is gracious and compassionate

PSALM 145:8-13

[8] Yahweh is gracious and compassionate,
slow to be angry and full of faithful love.
[9] Yahweh is good to all,
with compassion for all he has made.
[10] All you have made will praise you, O Yahweh,
your faithful will bless you;
[11] they will talk of your kingdom's glory,
and tell of your might,
[12] that all may know of your mighty deeds,
and your kingdom's glorious splendour.
[13] Your kingdom is a kingdom forever,
and your rule will last for all generations.
Yahweh keeps all his promises,
and shows faithful love to all he has made.

I thank you, O Lord, for your great love and tender compassion. Your goodness is endless and your gifts in creation are boundless. The whole universe gives you praise, and all your faithful people recount your blessings. Your kingdom is glorious and your rule is eternal. May all nations learn of your mighty acts and your constant love. I trust in your promises, O God, and I place myself in your care this day. Amen.

22 DECEMBER

Yahweh upholds all who fall

PSALM 145:14-21

[14] Yahweh upholds all who fall,
and all the bowed-down are raised up.
[15] All look to you in hope,
and you feed them with seasonal food.
[16] With open and generous hand
you meet the desires of all that live.
[17] Yahweh is just in all his ways
and faithful in all that he does.
[18] Yahweh is close to all who call to him,
to all who call to him in truth.
[19] He fulfils the desires of all who fear him,
and hears their cry and saves them.
[20] Yahweh guards all those who love him,
but sends the wicked to their doom.
[21] My mouth will speak in praise of Yahweh.
Let all that is made
bless his holy name forever and ever.

Raise me up in hope, O Lord, and grant me your abundant blessing this day. To live in your love is its own reward; and I pray that you will draw close to each and everyone of all your faithful people. I hold you in the deepest reverence, Lord, for your glory is scarcely to be imagined: but yet you know my every wish, and you guard my way. I will praise you forever. May the whole of creation praise your holy name. Amen.

23 DECEMBER

Do not put your trust in princes

PSALM 146:1-4

[1] Praise Yahweh!
Praise Yahweh, my soul!
[2] As long as I live I will praise Yahweh
I will praise Yahweh all my life,
I will sing praise to my God
as long as I live.
[3] Do not put your trust in princes,
in any person
with no power to save;
[4] when their spirits leave they go back to dust;
that very day
their plans come to nothing.

With my whole heart I praise you, O God, for you are mighty and above all earthly powers. Only in you do I put my trust, for even kings and princes are unreliable; but your promises are sure and your love is everlasting. All human powers will fail and even honest leaders will meet your judgement when they die. There is no certainty, O God, except in your promises. I praise your great and holy name. Amen.

24 DECEMBER

Yahweh upholds the cause of the oppressed

PSALM 146:5-10

[5] Blessed is he with Jacob's God to help him.
His hope is in Yahweh, his God,

[6] who made heaven, the earth,
the sea, and all in them.
He is faithful for evermore.
[7] He upholds the cause of the oppressed;
he gives food to the hungry.
Yahweh sets the prisoners free;
[8] Yahweh gives sight to the blind;
Yahweh lifts up the bowed-down;
Yahweh loves the upright;
[9] Yahweh protects the alien,
and sustains the orphan and widow
but thwarts the ways of the wicked.
[10] Yahweh will reign forever,
your God, O Zion, for all generations.
Praise Yahweh!

It was you who made the universe, O God, and you are the One who upholds it. May the hungry be fed and may the oppressed find justice. May those in prison be comforted and may those who cannot see receive your special grace. Protect those in need, Lord, and bring to nothing the plans of the unrighteous. Your reign is eternal. May all generations praise you. Amen.

25 DECEMBER

How good it is to sing psalms to our God

Psalm 147:1-6

[1] Praise Yahweh!
How good it is
to sing psalms to our God,
how pleasant and fitting to praise him!

[2] Yahweh rebuilds Jerusalem
and gathers the exiles of Israel.
[3] He heals the broken-hearted
and binds up their wounds.
[4] He fixes the number of stars
and gives each one a name.
[5] Yahweh is great and mighty in power,
and wise beyond any limits.
[6] Yahweh supports the poor
but brings the wicked to the ground.

O Lord, I love to sing your praises in the company of the faithful. Your works are wonderful to consider: you bring me back from the exile of my sin; you heal me when I am broken; you have set the stars in their courses; and your power is infinite. Give help to the needy, O Lord, and bring about the downfall of evil powers. I will sing your praises each day of my life. Amen.

26 DECEMBER

Sing to Yahweh a song of thanksgiving

PSALM 147:7-11

[7] Sing to Yahweh a song of thanksgiving;
play to our God on the harp.
[8] He covers the sky with clouds,
provides the earth with rain
and makes grass grow on the hills.
[9] He gives the food to the cattle
and the ravens' chicks when they caw.
[10] He takes no pride in the power of the horse,
nor pleasure in human strength;

[11] Yahweh delights in those who fear him,
who put their hope in his faithful love.

I give you thanks, O God, for all your wonderful gifts in creation. For your providential care in all aspects of life, I praise you. All powers in heaven and on earth come from you and any strength I may possess is your gift. I put all my hope in you, and I revere your holiness and majesty. I praise you with all my heart and soul, O Lord. Amen.

27 DECEMBER

Extol Yahweh, praise your God

PSALM 147:12-20

[12] Extol Yahweh, Jerusalem;
praise your God, O Zion.
[13] He gives strength to the bars of your gates,
he blesses your children within you.
[14] He keeps the peace of your borders
and gives you your fill
of finest wheat.
[15] He sends his word to the earth;
his command runs very swiftly;
[16] he spreads the snow like wool
and scatters frost like ashes;
[17] he hurls down hail like pebbles;
he sends the cold and the waters freeze.
[18] Then he sends his word and melts them;
he makes the wind blow and the waters flow.
[19] He reveals his word to Jacob,
his laws and decrees to Israel.

[20] He has done this for no other nation;
they do not know his decrees.
Praise Yahweh!

I thank you, O God, for your word in creation and for your revealed word in the scriptures. I praise you for the growth of your kingdom upon earth and I pray that all your faithful children may be strengthened by your grace. Bring peace among the nations and grant that the rich may learn to share with the poor and needy. Guide me, O Lord, until I reach the glorious gates of the heavenly Jerusalem. Amen.

28 DECEMBER

Praise Yahweh from the heavens

PSALM 148:1-6

[1] Praise Yahweh!
Praise Yahweh from the heavens;
praise him in the heights;
[2] praise him all his angels;
praise him all his heavenly throngs;
[3] praise him sun and moon;
praise him shining stars;
[4] praise him highest heavens,
and waters above the skies.
[5] Let them praise the name of Yahweh,
for he commanded and they were made;
[6] he fixed their place eternally,
by a law that will never end.

With the whole of heaven and earth I praise you, O Lord. My heart sings along with the host of your holy angels when I look upon the works of your hands. I praise you for making the sun and the moon; and for creating the myriads of stars which seem to stretch to infinity. I praise you for making nature's laws and for holding the foundations of the universe in place. I praise you mightily, O God. Amen.

29 DECEMBER

Praise Yahweh from earth

PSALM 148:7-14

[7] Praise Yahweh from earth:
sea monsters and ocean depths;
[8] lightning, hail, snow and clouds,
stormy wind that does his will;
[9] mountains and all hills,
fruit trees and cedars;
[10] wild beasts and cattle,
reptiles and flying birds;
[11] earth's kings and nations,
leaders and rulers of the world;
[12] young men and maidens,
old men and children.
[13] Let them praise the name of Yahweh;
his name is high above all others;
his splendour is higher
than earth and the heavens.
[14] He has made his people great in power,
he is the praise of all his faithful,
of Israel, the nation close to his heart.
Praise Yahweh!

I thank you for placing me upon this beautiful world, O God. I praise the loveliness of it all. The mountains, the oceans and the skies above reflect your glory. I pray that all the world's peoples will come to know you and will sing joyfully at the rich bounty of the earth. May the faithful praise you with thankfulness and may all nations worship you. Amen.

30 DECEMBER

Let the faithful exult in glory

PSALM 149

[1] Praise Yahweh!
Sing a new song to Yahweh,
his praise
in the assembly of the faithful.
[2] Let Israel rejoice in its maker,
let the people of Zion
rejoice in their King;
[3] let them praise his name
with dancing,
and play to him
on harp and tambourine;
[4] for Yahweh delights in his people,
and crowns the humble with victory.
[5] Let the faithful exult in glory,
and sing with joy on their couches;
[6] let them shout in praise of God,
and their hands wield a two-edged sword,
[7] to bring revenge on the nations,
and punishment on the peoples;
[8] to chain their kings in fetters,

and shackle their leaders with iron,
[9] to enforce the sentence against them,
to the glory of all his faithful! Praise Yahweh!

I will sing of your faithful love for the rest of my life, Lord. I praise your name and my spirit is filled with the music of angels. Your glory is marvellous to me and your majesty is beyond my understanding. Grant the faithful victory over evil powers and bring to judgement those who are wicked and cruel. Accept my praise and hear my prayer, O God. Amen.

31 DECEMBER

Praise Yahweh!

PSALM 150

[1] Praise Yahweh!
Praise God in his sanctuary;
praise him in his heavenly temple;
[2] praise him for his mighty deeds;
praise him for his measureless greatness.
[3] Praise him with trumpet fanfares;
praise him with harp and lyre;
[4] praise him with tambourine and dance;
praise him with strings and flute;
[5] praise him with cymbal clashes;
praise him with triumphant cymbal.
[6] Let everything that draws breath,
praise Yahweh!
Praise Yahweh!

I praise you with the company of the faithful, O God. I sing of your wondrous works and I recount your mighty deeds. Your love fills me to the brim and I am overflowing with your grace. Let the whole world sing with joy, for you are the King of the universe. Let all saints and angels shout with gladness, for you are King of heaven also. Let everything you have created praise you and thank you, O God, for you are the fountain of all that is. Amen.

PRAYING THE PSALMS WHATEVER THE OCCASION

Acclaim

for being the work of God's hands
14 January

for creation
7 March, 8 March, 28 August to 31 August, 1 September, 26 November, 29 November

for creatures
28 December, 29 December

for God's bounty
25 May

for God's power
25 February

for God's Word
5 February, 6 February, 9 October to 30 October

for history
22 June, 23 June, 9 July, 10 July, 2 September to 6 September, 25 November, 27 November, 28 November, 30 November

for the heavens
5 February

for the seas
4 August

Blessing

29 May, 30 May, 23 November, 24 November

A PSALM FOR SUNDAY

In praise of the Lord God

PSALM 148:1-4.7-13

[1] Praise Yahweh!
Praise Yahweh from the heavens;
praise him in the heights;
[2] praise him all his angels;
praise him all his heavenly throngs;
[3] praise him sun and moon;
praise him shining stars;
[4] praise him highest heavens,
and waters above the skies.
[7] Praise Yahweh from earth:
sea monsters and ocean depths;
[8] lightning, hail, snow and clouds,
stormy wind that does his will;
[9] mountains and all hills,
fruit trees and cedars;
[10] wild beasts and cattle,
reptiles and flying birds;
[11] earth's kings and nations,
leaders and rulers of the world,
[12] young men and maidens,
old men and children.
[13] Let them praise the name of Yahweh;
his name is high above all others;
his splendour is higher
than earth and the heavens.

A PSALM FOR MONDAY

Praise for the glories of creation

PSALM 104:1.4-5.12.14-15.19.24.27.30

[1] Praise Yahweh, my soul;
O Yahweh my God, how great you are,
clothed in splendour and majesty.
[4] Winds are his messengers
and flames of fire his servants.
[5] He fixed the earth on its foundations,
never to be moved.
[12] Birds of the air nest by the waters
and sing among the bushes.
[14] He provides the grass for cattle,
and plants for people to grow,
bringing food from the earth,
[15] wine to gladden people's hearts,
oil to make their faces glow,
and bread to feed their hearts.
[19] The moon marks the seasons
and the sun knows when to set.
[24] O Yahweh, your works are countless,
you made them all by your wisdom
and filled the earth with creatures.
[27] All these look to you for food
at the times when they need it.
[30] When you send your spirit life begins,
and you renew the face of the earth.

A PSALM FOR TUESDAY

In praise of the gift of life

PSALM 139:1-5.13-17.23-24

[1] You examined me, O Yahweh, and you know me.
[2] You know when I sit and when I rise;
you know my thoughts from afar off,
[3] you watch when I walk or lie down,
you know all the paths that I take.
[4] Before I have spoken a word,
O Yahweh, you know all about it.
[5] You keep close guard, behind and before me;
you spread your hand over me.
[13] For you made my innermost self;
you formed me in my mother's womb.
[14] I praise you because I am wonderfully made.
All that you do is wonderful;
that I know very well.
[15] Nothing about me was secret from you
when I was made in the secret place,
when I was formed in the depths of the earth.
[16] Your eyes could see my embryo.
All my days were inscribed in your book
before any one of them came to be.
[17] How mysterious, O God, are your thoughts to me;
how many they are!
[23] O God, examine me and know my heart,
test me, and know my anxious thoughts.
[24] See that my way does not lead to my ruin,
and guide me on the eternal road.

A PSALM, FOR WEDNESDAY

To put our life into perspective

PSALM 90:2-6.10.12.14

[2] Before the mountains were made,
before you formed the earth and the world,
you are God from eternity to eternity.
[3] You turn people back to dust,
saying, "Go back to dust,
you children of mortals",
[4] for in your sight a thousand years
are like a passing day,
are like an hour of night.
[5] You brush mortals away like a dream;
they are like the morning grass,
[6] which springs up new at dawn,
and withers dry by evening.
[10] Our span of life is seventy years,
or eighty if we have the strength,
but all that time is worry and trouble;
they quickly pass, and we fly away.
[12] Teach us to count our days,
that we may gain a wise heart.
[14] Each morning grant us your faithful love,
that we may sing for joy
and be glad all our days.

A PSALM FOR THURSDAY

Unbounded trust in the Lord

PSALM 121:1-8

[1] I lift up my eyes to the hills;
where will my help come from?
[2] My help comes from Yahweh,
who made heaven and earth.
[3] He will not allow your foot to slip;
your guardian will not slumber.
[4] The guardian of Israel
neither slumbers nor sleeps.
[5] Yahweh watches over you,
Yahweh, the shelter on your right;
[6] the sun will not harm you by day,
nor the moon by night.
[7] Yahweh will keep you from all harm,
he will guard your life;
[8] Yahweh will guard your coming and going,
both now and for eternity.

A PSALM FOR FRIDAY

For forgiveness of one's sins

Psalm 51:1-4.9-13

[1] Have mercy on me, O God, in your faithful love;
in your great compassion
blot out my offences.
[2] Wash away all my misdeeds,
and cleanse me from my sin.
[3] For I know my transgressions,
and my sin is always in my mind.
[4] I have sinned against you, only you,
and done what you see to be wrong;
you are justified in your sentence
and blameless in your judgement.
[9] Turn your face from my sins,
and blot out all my misdeeds.
[10] Create a pure heart in me, O God;
renew a resolute spirit in me.
[11] Do not thrust me from your presence;
do not remove your spirit of holiness.
[12] Give me back the joy of salvation;
sustain me with a willing spirit.
[13] Then I will teach transgressors your ways,
and sinners will come back to you.

A PSALM FOR SATURDAY

For a day of rest

PSALM 23:1-6

[1] My shepherd is Yahweh,
    I want for nothing.
[2] He lets me lie in fields of grass;
    he leads me by quiet streams
[3]   to revive my spirit
He guides me in paths of righteousness
    as befits his name.
[4] If I walked in the dark vale of death,
    I would fear no danger
    with you at my side;
your staff and crook both comfort me.
[5] You set a table for me
    in the presence of my foes;
you have poured fine oils on my head
    and my cup brims over.
[6] Goodness and faithful love
    will follow me all my life.
I make my home in Yahweh's house forever.